Data Acquisition Using LabVIEW

Transform physical phenomena into computer-acceptable data using a truly object-oriented language

Behzad Ehsani

BIRMINGHAM - MUMBAI

Data Acquisition Using LabVIEW

First published: December 2016

Production reference: 1121216

Published by Packt Publishing Ltd.
Livery Place
35 Livery Street
Birmingham
B3 2PB, UK.
ISBN 978-1-78217-216-1

www.packtpub.com

Credits

Author

Behzad Ehsani

Reviewer

Yik Yang

Commissioning Editor

Amarabha Banerjee

Acquisition Editor

Tushar Gupta

Content Development Editor

Narendrakumar Tripathi

Technical Editor

Anushree Arun Tendulkar

Copy Editor

Safis Editing

Project Coordinator

Devanshi Doshi

Proofreader

Safis Editing

Indexer

Tejal Daruwale Soni

Production Coordinator

Melwyn Dsa

About the Author

Behzad Ehsani is a computer engineering graduate who lives in the Silicon Valley in San Jose, California. He was born in Iran and came to the US with no money, planning to finish school in 4 years and go back to Iran as an engineer. That was 35 years ago! He worked night shifts at McDonald's and went to school in the morning. He recalls those years as a foggy dream (Fresno has foggy mornings). For all of those who remember what went on 35 years ago in Iran and the hostage crisis in US, it all may be (and, to an extent, is) the propaganda of one side or the other, but for Behzad, it had an immediate consequence. Being an Iranian was unimaginable during those years of his life, unimaginable in the sense that one would have to be in that position to know what each Iranian in the US, even those who had nothing to do with the events, had to endure. Immediately after the hostage crisis, Behzad had to drop out of university. After being fired from McDonald's for being an Iranian, he worked many blue-collar jobs, from pizza places to Italian restaurants and tutoring in first- and second-grade schools, and came to the conclusion that he should try his skills as a mechanic.

This was another turning point for him, since he soon met an American girlfriend in school, and the relationship ended with a citizenship after about 10 years. Behzad went back to his old routine; working at a gas station and going to school part time. He started studying electrical engineering. However, there was another revolution that took place: Sacramento State University was the first university that completely separated computer engineering from electrical engineering. Although it cost Behzad some units, he transferred his major to computer engineering. Connecting a telephone headset and a monitor to a central computer that took up several rooms was the most exciting thing for him. Many years later, personal computers were introduced, and Behzad describes opening a Mac SE with two floppies as one of the most delightful days of his life. Behzad was recruited as an engineer when Packard Bell opened a giant PC manufacturing company. While Behzad was in Sacramento, Silicon Valley was forming, and when he received a call from Apple Computers for a senior position, life became much better for him. Afterward, Behzad left Apple to work at Spectra Physics and, finally, he moved to work for Sentient Energy in Burlingame, by the San Francisco airport.

Acknowledgments

I am dedicating this book to my wife Susan Baradaran.

For without her love, tolerating my numerous mood changes (to anger) when things would not go my way.

For gradually changing our living room and kitchen table to a make messy lab.

For her calm and blind faith in me and my abilities.

I can not remember when I first seriously considered to actually write the book but I do remember well encouragements from my nephew Arash Kashani. I also should mention support of my family specially my mom and dad for without them in words of LabVIEW I would be "Device not found".

About the Reviewer

Yik Yang is a licensed professional engineer and a certified LabVIEW developer. He is the author of the *LabVIEW Graphical Programming Cookbook*. He has been working in the test and automation field for over 10 years in different industries: semiconductor, automotive, and power. Currently, he manages the validation and verification team for a company that designs and manufactures Smart-Grid Protection Systems.

www.PacktPub.com

For support files and downloads related to your book, please visit www.PacktPub.com.

Did you know that Packt offers eBook versions of every book published, with PDF and ePub files available? You can upgrade to the eBook version at www.PacktPub.com and as a print book customer, you are entitled to a discount on the eBook copy. Get in touch with us at service@packtpub.com for more details.

At www.PacktPub.com, you can also read a collection of free technical articles, sign up for a range of free newsletters and receive exclusive discounts and offers on Packt books and eBooks.

https://www.packtpub.com/mapt

Get the most in-demand software skills with Mapt. Mapt gives you full access to all Packt books and video courses, as well as industry-leading tools to help you plan your personal development and advance your career.

Why subscribe?

- Fully searchable across every book published by Packt
- Copy and paste, print, and bookmark content
- On demand and accessible via a web browser

Table of Contents

Preface

One of my most concerns, after finishing the book still is that the relationship of this book and the rest of the many of the other valuable functions is not appropriately mentioned.

What I would like from the readers to explore tons of videos and descriptions of functions from the `www.NI.com`.

Throughout the book I have tried to keep a balance between information for a novice to LabVIEW to intermediate user. I am came to this conclusion by more than a decade of working as design and automation and converting systems (hardware/software) from many other languages and hardware to products from National instruments mostly LabVIEW and and TestStand.

I believe I did not even use the word TestStand in the book; which I myself believe is an atrocity to such software and how one completes the other one. I did so because these systems are not explainable in words and only a book and accompanying videos can do the justice to LabVIEW and TestStand.

During last decade experience of mine with these software and hardware, there was not one manager that disagreed with me on recommendation of switching the existing system into LabVIEW and NI hardware.

I spent many days on the how the whole structure of the book should be. And if you read further you see that I used few actual hardware from NI than actually I would liked to. In my experience I noticed many works that the engineers had hacked some LabVIEW coed into languages like C or even basic. But this comes at a coast.

Being a completely GUI, LabVIEW has this images that many people look at a VI and say that "oh.. I can do this" but if similar code is shown to them in C or Basic, then the same people think twice.

Here lies the dichotomy. Cost versus practicality. LabVIEW is costly. While one can find many C compiler for free, it is sometimes hard to convince the upper management to migrate or start with LabVIEW. I found the best way to convince "finance" department is to make several simple and maybe some more complicated examples of the same program in both languages. I insist on this point strongly with a tiny "but".

The fact is that there is not one language that can be used everywhere. As we speak new languages are created and used.

With all I said, I mostly want to achieve two crucial points:

- My first choice to consider for any job would be LabVIEW
- LabVIEW is not appropriate for everything that exists out there

There is another important point that I would like to emphasize is that since LabVIEW is also attractive in appearance also, it influences a new graduate or a new engineer to cut short the homework that they must do.

LabVIEW does come with some standard functions, but unlike other languages, implementing a function that is written by an independent engineer is very simple. This is more important that it sounds.

It used to be a major technology change would come not shorter than 6 months. But now (2017) hardly anyone can keep up with the advances in their own expertise let alone what is going on the rest of the world of technology.

Importance of formal education

When I first got my engineering job at "Packard Bell" not to be confused "Hewlett Packard" I could not relate what we had learned in school and university with anything my manager wanted from me. This sounds like a contradiction with the title of this paragraph. But trust me they finally come together.

What I am trying to emphasize here is that do not take formal education lightly. National Instrument has training classes and if you are serious about learning LabVIEW and/or LabVIEW is your source of income, try your outmost to participate in formal education by NI.

TestStand

I have come to believe that one may get away by using LabVIEW in very high percentage of the jobs actual that is exist out there now (of corset hi is a relative statement) But there is a another software that complements LabVIEW very beautifully. The software is called TestStand and I have consciously have stayed away from TestStand both of these giant software and hardware that do require many books (at least two, one for each one) I strongly advice engineers that do automation tale a close look at the TestStand.

There is much help available

First of all like many other software companies, there is a technical help available from NI. In fact I believe one year of help is available with any purchase of LabVIEW. But also note that LabVIEW comes in more than one flavor choose the original version carefully.

What this book covers

Chapter 1, *LabVIEW Basics*, there is a brief introduction and a short note on installation. We will go over the most widely used pallets and objects Icon toolbar from a standard installation of LabVIEW and provide a brief explanation of what each object does.

Chapter 2, *The Most Common Communication Buses*, discusses the most common and practical ways we may communicate with external devices and collect data using LabVIEW.

Chapter 3, *Using the DAQ Assistant to Automatically Generate LabVIEW Code*, we use the automation capabilities of LabVIEW to create a VI that captures a triangular signal through simple DAQ hardware. We also use the DAQ Assistant VI to do almost all of the required programming.

Chapter 4, *DAQ Programming Using LabVIEW*, we started by defining what precisely the definition of data acquisition is. Further, we went through programs that actually used a programmable power supply and an oscilloscope where we set the power supply to specific values and measured the true output value of the power supply via an oscilloscope.

Chapter 5, *DAQ Debugging Techniques*, we have explored most, but not all debugging techniques that LabVIEW provides.

Chapter 6, *Real-World DAQ Programming Techniques*, focusses on minimal techniques that target a factory or a production environment.

Chapter 7, *Real-Time Issues*, discusses how to resolve upgradation issues.

Chapter 8, *DAQ at a Distance - Network and Distributed Systems*, shows how to use. Conet an ENET100 and we went through the connection step-by-step and verified each one.

Chapter 9, *Alternate Software for DAQ*, is about a second portion of powerful features provided within WebStorm. In this chapter, we focus on some of WebStorm's power features that help us boost productivity and developer experience.

Chapter 10, *Non-National Instrument Devices DAQ,* is about a second portion of powerful features provided within WebStorm. In this chapter, we focus on some of WebStorm's power features that help us boost productivity and developer experience.

Chapter 11, *LabVIEW and Simple Microcontrollers*, is about a second portion of powerful features provided within WebStorm. In this chapter, we focus on some of WebStorm's power features that help us boost productivity and developer experience.

What you need for this book

Refer to the LabVIEW Readme for more information on system requirements at `http://www.ni.com/pdf/manuals/374715f.html`. For latest information on LabVIEW you can visit `http://sine.ni.com/psp/app/doc/p/id/psp-357`.

Who this book is for

If you are an engineer, scientist, experienced hobbyist, or student, you will highly benefit from the content and examples illustrated in this book. A working knowledge of precision testing, measurement instruments, and electronics, as well as a background in computer fundamentals and programming is expected.

Conventions

In this book, you will find a number of text styles that distinguish between different kinds of information. Here are some examples of these styles and an explanation of their meaning.

Code words in text, database table names, folder names, filenames, file extensions, pathnames, dummy URLs, user input, and Twitter handles are shown as follows: "For example, a `while` loop can only be selected in Block Diagram"

New terms and **important words** are shown in bold. Words that you see on the screen, for example, in menus or dialog boxes, appear in the text like this: "To use an object, right-click inside the **Block Diagram** or **Front Panel** window, a pallet list appears."

Warnings or important notes appear in a box like this.

Tips and tricks appear like this.

Reader feedback

Feedback from our readers is always welcome. Let us know what you think about this book-what you liked or disliked. Reader feedback is important for us as it helps us develop titles that you will really get the most out of. To send us general feedback, simply e-mail feedback@packtpub.com, and mention the book's title in the subject of your message. If there is a topic that you have expertise in and you are interested in either writing or contributing to a book, see our author guide at www.packtpub.com/authors.

Customer support

Now that you are the proud owner of a Packt book, we have a number of things to help you to get the most from your purchase.

Downloading the example code

You can download the example code files for this book from your account at http://www.packtpub.com. If you purchased this book elsewhere, you can visit http://www.packtpub.com/support and register to have the files e-mailed directly to you.

You can download the code files by following these steps:

1. Log in or register to our website using your e-mail address and password.
2. Hover the mouse pointer on the **SUPPORT** tab at the top.
3. Click on **Code Downloads & Errata**.
4. Enter the name of the book in the **Search** box.
5. Select the book for which you're looking to download the code files.
6. Choose from the drop-down menu where you purchased this book from.
7. Click on **Code Download**.

Once the file is downloaded, please make sure that you unzip or extract the folder using the latest version of:

- WinRAR / 7-Zip for Windows
- Zipeg / iZip / UnRarX for Mac
- 7-Zip / PeaZip for Linux

The code bundle for the book is also hosted on GitHub at `https://github.com/PacktPubl ishing/Data-Acquisition-Using-LabVIEW`. We also have other code bundles from our rich catalog of books and videos available at `https://github.com/PacktPublishing/`. Check them out!

Downloading the color images of this book

We also provide you with a PDF file that has color images of the screenshots/diagrams used in this book. The color images will help you better understand the changes in the output. You can download this file from `https://www.packtpub.com/sites/default/files/down loads/DataAcquisitionUsingLabVIEW_ColorImages.pdf`.

Errata

Although we have taken every care to ensure the accuracy of our content, mistakes do happen. If you find a mistake in one of our books-maybe a mistake in the text or the code-we would be grateful if you could report this to us. By doing so, you can save other readers from frustration and help us improve subsequent versions of this book. If you find any errata, please report them by visiting `http://www.packtpub.com/submit-errata`, selecting your book, clicking on the **Errata Submission Form** link, and entering the details of your errata. Once your errata are verified, your submission will be accepted and the errata will be uploaded to our website or added to any list of existing errata under the Errata section of that title.

To view the previously submitted errata, go to `https://www.packtpub.com/books/conten t/support` and enter the name of the book in the search field. The required information will appear under the **Errata** section.

Piracy

Piracy of copyrighted material on the Internet is an ongoing problem across all media. At Packt, we take the protection of our copyright and licenses very seriously. If you come across any illegal copies of our works in any form on the Internet, please provide us with the location address or website name immediately so that we can pursue a remedy.

Please contact us at `copyright@packtpub.com` with a link to the suspected pirated material.

We appreciate your help in protecting our authors and our ability to bring you valuable content.

Questions

If you have a problem with any aspect of this book, you can contact us at `questions@packtpub.com`, and we will do our best to address the problem.

1
LabVIEW Basics

In this chapter, after a brief introduction and a short note on installation, we will go over the most widely used pallets and objects Icon toolbar from a standard installation of **LabVIEW** and provide a brief explanation of what each object does. We will end the chapter with an example of a LabVIEW program generally called a **Virtual Instrument (VI)**.

Introduction to LabVIEW

LabVIEW is a graphical developing and testing environment unlike any other test and development tool available in the industry. LabVIEW sets itself apart from traditional programming environments by its completely graphical approach to programming. As an example, while representation of a `while` loop in a text-based language such as C consists of several predefined, extremely compact, and sometimes extremely cryptic lines of text, a `while` loop in LabVIEW is actually a graphical loop. The environment is extremely intuitive and powerful, which makes for a short learning curve for the beginner. LabVIEW is based on what is called the G language, but there are still other languages, especially C, under the hood. However, the ease of use and power of LabVIEW is somewhat deceiving to a novice user. Many people have attempted to start projects in LabVIEW only because, at first glance, the graphical nature of the interface and the concept of drag and drop used in LabVIEW appears to do away with the required basics of programming concepts and classical education in programming science and engineering. This is far from the reality of using LabVIEW as the predominant development environment. While it is true that, in many higher-level development and testing environments, especially when using complicated test equipment and complex mathematical calculations or even creating embedded software, LabVIEW's approach will be a much more time-efficient and bug-free environment which otherwise would require several lines of code in a traditional text based programming environment, one must be aware of LabVIEW's strengths and possible weaknesses.

LabVIEW does not completely replace the need for traditional text based languages and, depending on the entire nature of a project, LabVIEW or another traditional text based language such as C may be the most suitable programming or test environment.

Installing LabVIEW

Installation of LabVIEW is very simple and it is just as routine as any modern-day program installation; that is, insert the DVD 1 and follow the onscreen guided installation steps.

LabVIEW comes in one DVD for the Mac and Linux versions but in four or more DVDs for the Windows edition (depending on additional software, different licensing, and additional libraries and packages purchased). In this book, we will use the **LabVIEW 2013 Professional Development** version for Windows. Given the target audience of this book, we assume the user is fully capable of installing the program. Installation is also well documented by **National Instruments** (**NI**) and the mandatory 1-year support purchase with each copy of LabVIEW is a valuable source of live and e-mail help. Also, the NI website (www.ni.com) has many user support groups that are also a great source of support, example codes, discussion groups, local group events and meetings of fellow LabVIEW developers, and so on.

It's worth noting for those who are new to the installation of LabVIEW that the installation DVDs include much more than what an average user would need and pay for. We do strongly suggest that you install additional software (beyond what has been purchased and licensed or immediately needed!). This additional software is fully functional in demo mode for 7 days, which may be extended for about a month with online registration. This is a very good opportunity to have hands-on experience with even more of the power and functionality that LabVIEW is capable of offering. The additional information gained by installing the other software available on the DVDs may help in further development of a given project. Just imagine, if the current development of a robot only encompasses mechanical movements and sensors today, optical recognition is probably going to follow sooner than one may think. If data acquisition using expensive hardware and software may be possible in one location, the need for web sharing and remote control of the setup is just around the corner. It is very helpful to at least be aware of what packages are currently available and be able to install and test them prior to a full purchase and implementation. The following screenshot shows what may be installed if almost all the software on all the DVDs is selected:

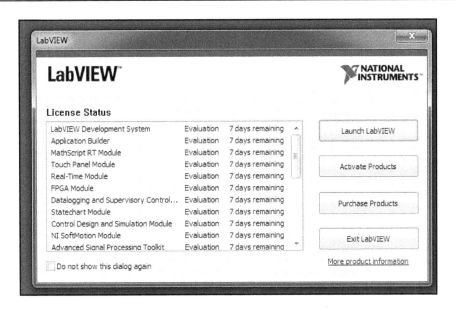

When installing a fresh version of LabVIEW, if you do decide to observe the given advice, make sure to click on the + sign next to each package you decide to install and prevent any installation of `LabWindows/CVI...` and `Measurement Studio... for Visual Studio`. LabWindows, according to NI, is an ANSI C integrated development environment. Also note that, by default, NI device drivers are not selected to be installed. Device drivers are an essential part of any data acquisition and appropriate drivers for communications and instrument(s) control must be installed before LabVIEW can interact with external equipment. Also, note that device drivers (on Windows installations) come on a separate DVD, which means that one does not have to install device drivers at the same time that the main application and other modules are installed; they can be installed at any time later on. Almost all well-established vendors are packaging their product with LabVIEW drivers and example codes. If a driver is not readily available, NI has programmers that would do just that. But this would come at a cost to the user.

VI Package Manager, now installed as a part of standard installation, is also a must these days. NI distributes third-party software and drivers and public domain packages via VI Package Manager. We are going to use examples using Arduino (`http://www.arduino.cc`) microcontrollers in later chapters of this book. Appropriate software and drivers for these microcontrollers are installed via VI Package Manager. You can install many public domain packages that further install many useful LabVIEW toolkits to a LabVIEW installation and can be used just as those that are delivered professionally by NI.

Finally, note that the more modules, packages, and software that are selected to be installed, the longer it will take to complete the installation. This may sound like making an obvious point but, surprisingly enough, installation of all software on the three DVDs (for Windows) takes up over 5 hours! On a standard laptop or PC we used. Obviously, a more powerful PC (such as one with a solid state hard drive) may not take such long time.

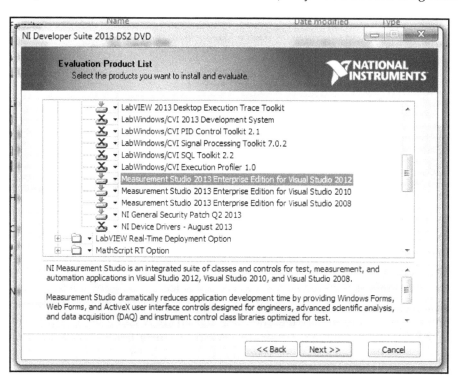

A basic LabVIEW VI

Once the LabVIEW application is launched, by default two blank windows open simultaneously–a **Front Panel** and a **Block Diagram** window–and a VI is created:

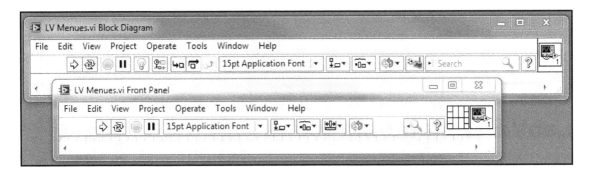

VIs are the heart and soul of LabVIEW. They are what separate LabVIEW from all other text-based development environments. In LabVIEW, everything is an object which is represented graphically. A VI may only consist of a few objects or hundreds of objects embedded in many *subVIs*. These graphical representations of a thing, be it a simple `while` loop, a complex mathematical concept such as Polynomial Interpolation, or simply a Boolean constant, are all graphically represented. To use an object, right-click inside the **Block Diagram** or **Front Panel** window, a pallet list appears. Follow the arrow and pick an object from the list of objects from subsequent pallet and place it on the appropriate window. The selected object can now be dragged and placed on different locations on the appropriate window and is ready to be wired. Depending on what kind of object is selected, a graphical representation of the object appears on both windows. Of course, there are many exceptions to this rule. For example, a `while` loop can only be selected in **Block Diagram** and, by itself, a `while` loop does not have a graphical representation on the **Front Panel** window. Needless to say, LabVIEW also has keyboard combinations that expedite selecting and placing any given toolkit objects onto the appropriate window:

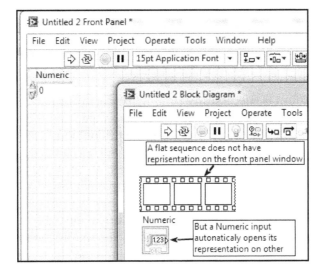

Each object has one (or several) wire connections going into it as input(s) and coming out as its output(s). A VI becomes functional when a minimum number of wires are appropriately connected to the input and output of one or more objects. Later, we will use an example to illustrate how a basic LabVIEW VI is created and executed.

LabVIEW menu bar icons

A few words about menu bar icons are necessary. Note that actual menus and submenus do the main work and one must be familiarized with the functionality of many menus and their subsequent submenus and panels. The following are the absolutely necessary items a user must be familiar with to begin work in LabVIEW.

- The Run button will commence execution of a VI given that a minimum of code is provided at least in the Block Diagram window. A few points must be noted:
    - A program may have enough code and this button may be pressed but there may not be anything obvious or present in any of the open windows
    - A program or a VI may run perfectly fine and extremely fast, as fast as the speed of the computer that LabVIEW is running on (given all operating system delays, background programs and processes, and so on) without anything noticeable to the human eye. Care must be taken to spot insert alerts, delays, or indicators if needs be.

- When a program is successfully running (independent of the actual intended objective of the VI) these four Icons change shape from their idle state appearance. Note that there may be unintentional loops that will appear as "successful running program to LabVIEW" such as a `while` loop that does not have correct exit condition(s), typically called an endless loop. In such a case (where even milliseconds of delay is not implemented), LabVIEW would get hold of all processors on the computer and may lock the computer such that no buttons on LabVIEW or, for that matter, even keyboard and mouse clicks would be effective. In these cases, depending on the operating system in use, a user may have to temporarily shut down the computer to be able to escape from the locked-up situation. LabVIEW precompiles as objects are placed on the programming windows; this is an important fact that a user must keep in mind and although it is an obvious benefit, it may unintentionally work against the user if proper care is not taken while designing and implementing a project.

- The broken link error changes the shape of the Run button. The Run button will change shape to this form if:
    - Not enough inputs and/or outputs are correctly wired
    - There are connections errors
    - An unwired object is placed in any of the two main windows of a VI

- The Run continuously state is shown as follows.

- The Run continuously (active) button (two looping arrows) will execute a VI over and over even though the actual VI logic has not provisioned to run more than once. Used with caution, this button is a good way of running/testing a code segment (such as a subVI) which may be planned to be incorporated in a looped project.

- The Stop button.

- The Pause button.

- The highlight execution button may be the quickest and the most useful way of debugging or simply viewing the actual sequence of execution of each object and the value carried by a wire or output of a function. When evoked prior to clicking the Run button, LabVIEW slows down the execution of program such that a moving dot, and most likely several moving dots on different wires, on the currently executing wire is traceable by human eye and speed.

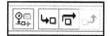

- Debug tools, start single stepping(s) and step out.

- Arrange tools. LabVIEW is graphical programming environment (although scripts may be used inside a few functions) and, as such, proper arranging of graphical representation of each object is essential to a readable and manageable source code. These buttons are very helpful in arranging and aligning groups of objects.

- There are many occasions that an object must move to the back or to the front of a layered segment; the Reorder button arranges buttons with respect to layers rather than the position of an object in a given layer. Mostly used in the decorative aspect of a **Front Panel** window.

- Any VI is created by manually placing an object onto its respective window and probably resizing it (such as a `for` loop or a `while` loop) and all objects need to be manually wired. Even on a simple VI, this process may get overwhelmingly complicated and it is very hard to trace each wire from where it starts to where it ends. Clean Up can actually help to automatically rearrange a complete VI or a selected segment of the code. However, save the code before applying automatic Clean Up to your code since there exist situations where a Clean Up may make the **Block Diagram** *prettier* but may also cause the code to be harder to read and/or add or remove any of its objects. With little experience and continuous and periodic applications of Clean Up, this could become a very useful tool.

- Activating the Help button and hovering over any object will automatically open a window with very helpful information about that object, related documents, and even links to examples and usage information.

- The Connector pane icon object is used to connect wires to input of this subVI and/or have access to its output(s) if either case does exist.

- Icon editing tool, by default, any new VI has this icon and only the subsequent numbers on the bottom right of the icon are enumerated. By clicking on this tool, an Icon editor subprogram is launched where users can create and edit their own icons or import previously created icons.

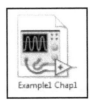

- When a VI is created, the actual file is represented by this icon, which can also be modified by an editor.

Example 1 – counter with a gauge

This is a fairly simple program with simple user interaction. Once the program has been launched, it uses a `while` loop to wait for the user input. This is a typical behavior of almost any user-friendly program. For example, if the user launches Microsoft Office, the program launches and waits for the user to pick a menu item, click on a button, or perform any other action that the program may provide. Similarly, this program starts execution but waits in a loop for the user to choose a command. In this case only a simple Start or Stop is available. If the Start button is clicked, the program uses a `for` loop function to simply count from 0 to 10 in intervals of 200 milliseconds. After each count is completed, the gauge on the **Front Panel**, the GUI part of the program, is updated to show the current count. The counter is then set to the zero location of the gauge and the program awaits subsequent user input. If the Start button is clicked again, this action is repeated, and, obviously, if the Stop button is clicked, the program exits. Although very simple, in this example, you can find many of the concepts that are often used in a much more elaborate program. Let's walk through the code and point out some of these concepts.

The following steps not only walk the reader through the example code but are also a brief tutorial on how to use LabVIEW, how to utilize each working window, and how to wire objects.

Launch LabVIEW and from the **File** menu, choose **New VI** and follow the steps:

1. Right-click on the **Block Diagram** window.
2. From **Programming Functions**, choose **Structures** and select **While Loop**.
3. Click (and hold) and drag the cursor to create a (resizable) rectangle.
4. On the bottom-left corner, right-click on the wire to the stop loop and choose **Create a control**. Note that a Stop button appears on both the **Block Diagram** and **Front panel** windows.
5. Inside the `while` loop box, right-click on the **Block Diagram** window and from **Programming Function**, choose **Structures** and select **Case Structures**. Click and (and hold) and drag the cursor to create a (resizable) rectangle.

6. On the `Front Panel` window, next to the Stop button created, right-click and from **Modern Controls**, choose **Boolean** and select an **OK** button. Double-click on the text label of the **OK** button and replace the **OK** button text with `Start`. Note that an **OK** button is also created on the **Block Diagram** window and the text label on that button also changed when you changed the text label on the **Front Panel** window.

7. On the **Front Panel** window, drag-and-drop the newly created **Start** button next to the tiny green question mark on the left-hand side of the **Case Structure** box, outside of the case structure but inside the `while` loop. Wire the **Start** button to the **Case Structure**.

8. Inside the **Case Structure** box, right-click on the **Block Diagram** window and from **Programming Function**, choose **Structures** and select **For Loop**. Click and (and hold) and drag the cursor to create a (resizable) rectangle.

9. Inside the **Case Structure** box, right-click on **N** on the top-left side of the **Case Structure** and choose **Create Constant**. An integer blue box with a value of **0** will be connected to the For Loop. This is the number of irritations the `for` loop is going to have. Change 0 to 11.

10. Inside the For Loop box, right click on the **Block Diagram** widow and from **Programming Function**, choose Timing and select Wait(ms).

11. Right-click on the **Wait** function created in step 10 and connect a integer value of 200 similar to step 9.

12. On the **Front Panel** window, right-click and from **Modern functions**, choose **Gauge**. Note that a **Gauge** function will appear on the **Block Diagram** window too. If the function is not inside the **For Loop**, drag and drop it inside the **For Loop**.

13. Inside the **For loop**, on the **Block Diagram** widow, connect the iteration count i to the **Gauge**.

14. On the **Block Diagram**, right-click on the **Gauge**, and under the **Create** submenu, choose **Local** variable.

15. If it is not already inside the `while` loop, drag and drop it inside the `while` loop but outside of the case structure.

16. Right-click on the local variable created in step 15 and connect a Zero to the input of the local variable.

17. Click on the Clean Up icon on the main menu bar on the **Block Diagram** window and drag and move items on the **Front Panel** window so that both windows look similar to the following screenshots:

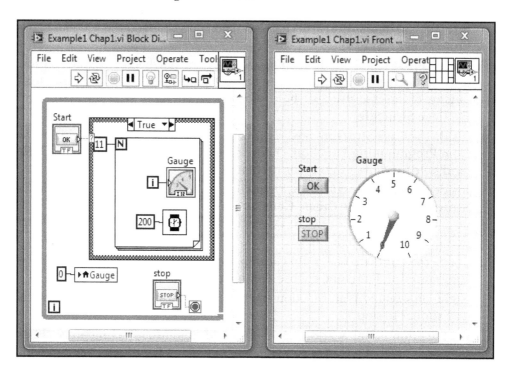

Creating a project is a must

When LabVIEW is launched, a default screen such as in the following screenshot appears on the screen:

The most common way of using LabVIEW, at least in the beginning of a small project or test program, is to create a new VI. A common rule of programming is that each function, or in this case VI, should not be larger than a page. Keep in mind that, by nature, LabVIEW will have two windows to begin with and, being a graphical programming environment only, each VI may require more screen space than the similar text based development environment. To start off development and in order to set up all devices and connections required for tasks such as data acquisition, a developer may get the job done by simply creating one, and, more likely several VIs. Speaking from experience among engineers and other developers (in other words, in situations where R&D looms more heavily on the project than collecting raw data), quick VIs are more efficient initially, but almost all projects that start in this fashion end up growing very quickly and other people and other departments will need be involved and/or be fed the gathered data. In most cases, within a short time from the beginning of the project, technicians from the same department or related teams may be need to be trained to use the software in development. This is why it is best to develop the habit of creating a new project from the very beginning. Note the center button on the left-hand window in the preceding screenshot.

Creating a new project (as opposed to creating VIs and sub-VIs) has many advantages and it is a must if the program created will have to run as an executable on computers that do not have LabVIEW installed on them. Later versions of LabVIEW have streamlined the creation of a project and have added many templates and starting points to them.

Although, for the sake of simplicity, we created our first example with the creation of a simple VI, one could almost as easily create a project and choose from many starting points, templates, and other concepts (such as architecture) in LabVIEW.

The most useful starting point for a complete and user-friendly application for data acquisition would be a state machine. Throughout the book, we will create simple VIs as a quick and simple way to illustrate a point but, by the end of the book, we will collect all of the VIs, icons, drivers, and sub-VIs in one complete state machine, all collected in one complete project.

From the project created, we will create a standalone application that will not need the LabVIEW environment to execute, which could run on any computer that has LabVIEW runtime engine installed on it.

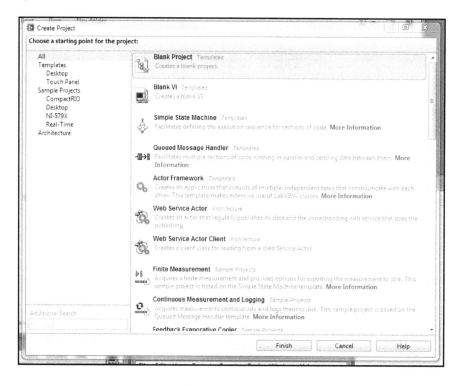

Chapter highlights

LabVIEW is a complete object-oriented development and test environment based on the G language. As such, it is a very powerful and complex environment. In this chapter, we went through an introduction to LabVIEW and the main functionality of each of its icons by way of an actual user-interactive example. Accompanied by appropriate hardware (both NI as well as many industry standard test, measurement, and development hardware products), LabVIEW is capable of covering developing embedded systems, fuzzy logic, and almost everything in between!

Summary

In this chapter, we covered the basics of LabVIEW, from installation to an in-depth explanation of each and every element in the toolbar.

In the next chapter, we will discuss the most common and practical ways we may connect the computer which LabVIEW is running on to the device(s) we need to collect data from.

2
Most Common Communication Buses

In this chapter, we will discuss the most common and practical ways we may communicate with external devices and collect data using LabVIEW. Device connections are dependent on at least two parameters–the communication bus (serial, USB, GPIB, I2C, and so on) and the connection medium (single wire, a cable).

Wired connections and drivers

Automatic data acquisition would require a complete or at least a partially functioning system. At best, according to IEEE guidelines, a device may only respond when it is asked to perform a task. While this may be the ideal case, we are often dealing with systems that are sending continuous streams of data. We use the word *system* to define a set of device(s) that include at least one sensor, or an instrument such as an oscilloscope, a power supply, and so on, which is connected to a computer running LabVIEW via a physical connector. Granted, on a more advanced systems, data acquisition may be accomplished through wireless connections (still, in almost all cases, a system would need an intermediate physical layer between a computer and a wireless communication device). But for all practical purposes, let us start with what is most commonly used in the industry or perhaps a university lab. Needless to say, any communications established within a system must be based on some existing or in-development and/or proprietary bus or protocol. In almost all cases (particularly on the Windows operating system), installation of device drivers is not to be taken lightly. Many common errors are driver-related.

If you have not done so already, please find the latest serial drivers from the NI website and install them. If you are using a measurement instrument such as an oscilloscope, a power supply, or a current meter as a part of your test or data acquisition system, download and install the appropriate drivers from `http://www.ni.com`(or a third-party device manufacturer). NI usually provides two types of certified drivers for a given instrument–a **Plug and Play** (**PnP**) and a project-style driver. Depending on which version you may want to use, the complete driver folder would reside in a specific path in your `National Instruments` folder. A project style instrument driver would need to be placed in `<LabVIEW>\instr.lib`.

Serial communication

A 1-Wire®, or most probably a 3-wire (signal ground, receive, and transmit), serial over USB accounts for one of the oldest and still most common forms of communication between a device and a data acquisition subsystem (a computer running LabVIEW in our case). Do not forget power and ground wires also. Since data acquisition is our focus in this book, we will somewhat leap over a 1-wire connection but it is worth mentioning that an amazing amount of communication can be achieved on a 1-wire serial connection. For example, a 1-wire digital temperature sensor, DS18B20, will send a unique serial number along with the actual data requested every time a set of data is transmitted. So you may use several of these temperature sensors (even 50, if you need them all) and still distinguish the exact pair of data and serial number for each sensor, all by using only one digital serial bus pin. As simple and friendly serial communication is, it is one of the slowest forms of communication. Also, there is a another drawback with serial communication: the integrity of the data gathered through serial communication is not guaranteed.

Almost all devices that I have worked with use serial communication, even those which have USB ports. One may use serial through USB. Note that during the development of a device, resource allocation between development and testing is very fluent. A device goes through no testing (at the beginning, simply because there is nothing to test) and as the device matures, less development and more and more testing becomes necessary.

FTDI USB RS232 and TTL level serial to USB cables are also one of the most widely used converters. This family of converters have drivers for all three major platforms (Windows, Mac OS, and Linux) and many others such as the Android platform, which makes them very popular in almost any embedded and hardware level data acquisition and development environment. Refer to `http://www.ftdichip.com`for a complete list of serial to USB converters and corresponding drivers. Also note the new low (3.3 voltage) support:

This is a USB to FTDI cable	

GPIB

During the 1960s, long before USB, USB2, and now USB type-C dominated the bus systems on most platforms and appeared as the built-in standard on all desktop computers and laptops, a digital communication standard, originally developed by HP, was registered as an IEEE 488.x standard. This standard, also called **General Purpose Interface Bus** (**GPIB**), is still widely used and well in existence (many were sold several years back) in the test and development industry and many university labs.

We will also use an NI GPIB-USB-HS, a GPIB to USB converter to connect a Tektronix TDS 2022 to the PC running LabVIEW. Don't forget that this particular converter, or similar products manufactured by other vendors, also needs special drivers. NI provides proprietary drivers for GPIB-USB-HS (found on `http://www.ni.com/`). A GPIB to UB converter is also available from HP (Agilent) that may be used directly in LabVIEW:

GPIB to USB converter	

It's worth noting that Intel/Apple computers have been working on standards that are much faster than the latest and fastest original USB. See the following table for a quick comparison:

Type	Max speed (bytes per second)
USB 1.1	1.5 MBps
USB 2	60 MBps
USB 3.0	625 MBps
USB 3.1	1.21 GBps
Thunderbolt	1.2 Bps (two channels)

Thunderbolt 2	2.5 GBps
Thunderbolt 3	40 GBps

Note that in order to use an HP (Agilent) GPIB converter, special drivers from HP must also be installed on top of the NI drivers and (very importantly) the passport option in LabVIEW must be turned on, before LabVIEW can directly use a converter made by HP (Agilent).

SCPI commands sets

As more and more test instruments using different buses and protocols entered engineering and test labs, a need for standard and *universal* sets of commands, as well as syntax and data formats to program and automate these devices, became a necessity. In 1990, IEEE 488.2 completed the standard that started with IEEE 488.1. This standard covers classes of instruments as well of product-specific commands. Although this standard was originally designed to accommodate a GPIB bus using ASCII text strings, it can also be used in USB, Serial and RS232 and Ethernet other lesser known architectures.

As an example, if we look down in the lower levels of NI drivers and examples to automate a Tektronix TD 2022, we will find standard SCPI commands:

SCPI commands

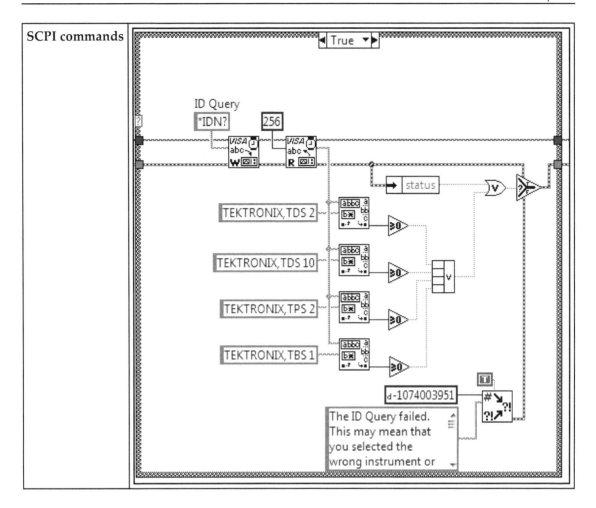

Arduino for LabVIEW driver installation

Arduino and its compatible boards and shields are an open source class of products (hardware as well as software), the most common of which is a microcontroller called **Arduino Uno**. This microcontroller is built around an ATmega328 with plenty of digital and analog I/O pins. National Instruments (unofficially) supports Arduino and Arduino-compatible devices and shields through a special firmware and set of functions. To illustrate the power and ease of use of these microcontrollers, as an example, we will use an Arduino Uno. Please refer to https://www.arduino.cc/ and the instructions on http://ni.com under LabVIEW interface for Arduino toolkit using **VI Package Manager** (**VIPM**) to install all provided functions via the Internet. Go to http://vipm.jki.net/ to get VIMP (there is a free version).

Once properly installed, you should see a function plate such as the one depicted in the following screenshot in your function panel list. To emphasize the importance of communications and the correct installation of drivers, I will warn you that special firmware (available from the NI LabVIEW site) and this part of the installation must be done through the *Arduino IDE before anything else will work*. Unless you are very careful to follow instructions properly, then I am pretty sure that you will get `Error 5003` that indicates not all software drivers are correctly installed.

In the following screenshot, you can see the function pallet of the LabVIEW Arduino-compatible functions and drivers window:

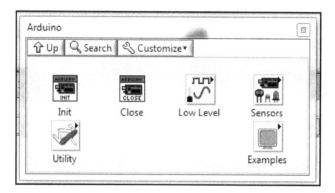

Arduino photo sensor board

We are now ready to go through an example. The purpose of this example is to illustrate that finding and installing libraries and drivers is a routine part of data acquisition. Arduino sensor kits provide about 40 boards and sensors for about $40 from Amazon (for example) but if you spend the required time and effort, you may buy the same sensor packs much cheaper on eBay or other resellers found on the internet. Complete source code and pictures of the Front Panel and Block Diagram are provided. The aim is to have the reader acquire and install the rest (IDE, drivers, and firmware) to emphasize the fact that nowadays most of the drivers and the latest instructions for almost any instrument reside on the internet and diver hunting and installing is an "art" that must be simultaneously acquired during learning data acquisition!!

In this example, we will use the following:

- An Arduino Uno R3:

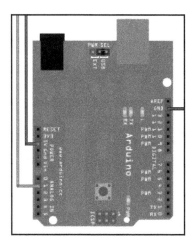

- A photo resistor sensor board:

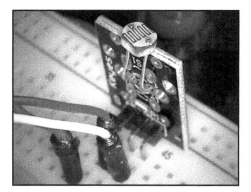

Hardware connection:

1. Connect the center pin of the sensor board to 5V on Arduino.
2. Connect the pin marked S on the sensor to IO 1 of the Arduino.
3. Connect the pin marked as (-) to ground on Arduino.

4. Open LabVIEW and create the circuit here:

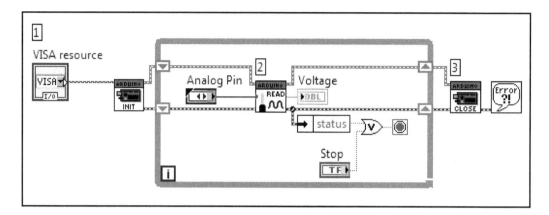

You should have a front panel like (or very similar to) this:

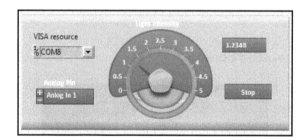

Run the program. Shine light on the sensor (or block light going to the sensor) and notice the dial movement.

If you get errors, make sure you are using the correct port and the correct pin on the analog in (on the Arduino board).

Summary

From a 1-wire® serial communication to a GPIB connection cable with at least 24 wires, to a USB to Serial connector, and so on, the choice of using one particular connecting wire or cable over another one or, on the other hand, the availability of certain bus on a computer or a standalone test system may vary depending on at what stage of development (R&D, development, or production) we may be. The choice of connection cable/adapter device will also will have a decisive effect on the data transfer rate. The data transfer rate could be the single deciding factor with which a connection bus may have to be used. Clearly, a GPIB data transfer rate is much higher than a simple serial data transfer rate. The format of the data acquired (numbers, text, wave form, and so on) is also fundamental to data acquisition. We will look at I2C, 1-wire or 3 wire Serial, RS232, GPIB and USB, and, in particular, virtual serial port(s) using a USB connection in upcoming chapters.

3
Using the DAQ Assistant to Automatically Generate LabVIEW Code

The ease of use and GUI interface of LabVIEW makes it an ideal candidate for test and data acquisition automation in general, but LabVIEW has built-in automation *express* VIs that make the process of automation even easier. In this chapter, we will use an **NI USB 6008**, a simple USB **data acquisition** (**DAQ**) device, and the DAQ assistant express VI to see how we can utilize the auto code generation of LabVIEW to acquire external data. We will use a function generator to create a triangular wave and capture the output both graphically and numerically in LabVIEW.

Capturing a triangular signal

To demonstrate one simple aspect of LabVIEW automation, we will attempt to capture a triangular waveform created by a function generator. We will connect an FG085 function generator directly to a DAQ (NI USB 6008). The function generator will create a triangular wave form and we will capture this wave both graphically, on the front panel window of LabVIEW, and also save the data collected in a separate file for later use and analysis.

Devices required

We will use the following:

- National Instrument USB 6008:

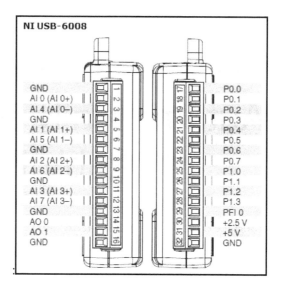

USB 6008 DAQ is a low-cost multifunction DAQ. As the name implies, this DAQ connects to the PC via a USB bus. Connect the USB DAQ to the PC using a USB cable. Note the auto recognition of the device by the computer on the taskbar. If all goes well, the green LED next to the input cable will blink continuously. If the drivers are not already installed, use the CD accompanying the DAQ to install the divers. It is best to check the National Instruments website to make sure that you have the latest version of the driver.

Note: It is imperative to make certain that the USB DAQ is correctly recognized by the PC running LabVIEW. One way to verify this is to look at the Device Manager under the Control Panel of Windows. If you cannot see the device in the list of devices under Device Manager, check the connections and cables, and, most importantly, verify that you have installed the correct device drivers for the specific device you are using.

You can also use **NI MAX** to do the same job of finding your devices and drivers.

- Analog inputs: 8 SE/4 DIFF 10 kS/s 12 bits
- Analog outputs: 2 150 S/s 12 bits

- Digital I/O: 12 DIO Counter/Timers: 1 32 bits 5 MHz
- Measurement type: Voltage:

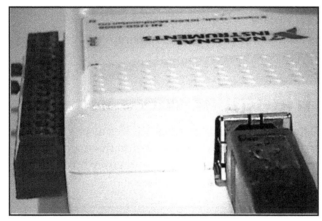

LabVIEW will present device pin-out automatically for NI devices. This function is available through NI MAX (we will discuss NI MAX in detail in upcoming chapters). In this example, we will use analog input AI0. Connect the signal generator wires directly to AI0 on the USB DAQ.

To generate the desired waveform, we will also use a function generator (in this example, we are using **FG085 miniDDS Function Generator**):

Refer to your function generator setup manual to set the following on your particular function generator:

1. Set frequency to 10.0KHz
2. Set amplitude to 3.0V
3. DC offset is not our concern at this moment

Capturing triangular wave VI

We will use DAQ assistant, which is an **express VI**, in this example. Unlike other VIs, an express VI contains scripts and automation that guide the user through different windows to make appropriate changes to various settings and entry boxes to customize the VI to manage one or several inputs and outputs and tasks:

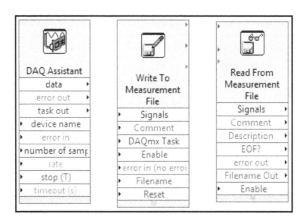

Perform the following steps:

1. Launch LabVIEW and create a new VI, choose an appropriate name for it, and save the VI.
2. Right-click on the **Block Diagram** window of the newly created VI and, from **Measurement I/O**, click on **NI-DAQmax** and choose **DAQ Assist**, and place it on the **Block Diagram** window:

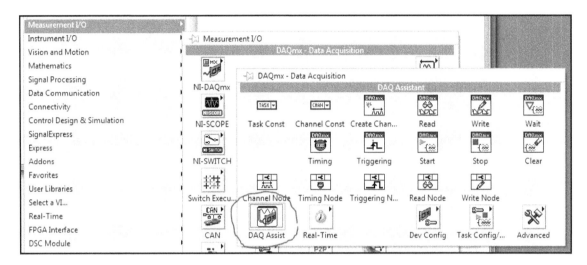

3. Once the function is placed on the window, quick *initialization* will take place:

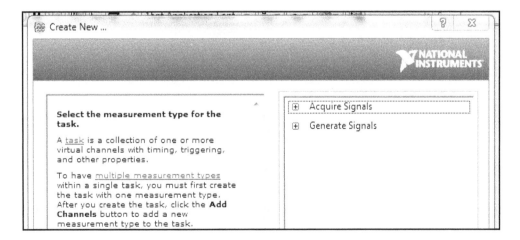

4. The next screen will present you with two choices. Note the plus (**+**) signs next to **Acquire Signals** and **Generate Signals**. We are going to acquire a voltage signal. Click on the plus sign next to **Acquire Signals** then click on the (**+**) next to **Analog Inputs** and select **Voltage**.

   A physical channels selection window will appear. Note that at this time LabVIEW is aware of what hardware is actually connected to your computer and it is presenting you with available channels based on previous selection. In our example, we only have one device (**USB-6008**) and we have eight available analog inputs. Remember that we connected the signal generator to ai0. Select **ai0** and click on **Finish**:

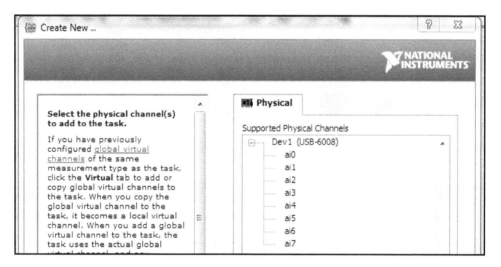

5. The next window that is presented is the actual **DAQ Assistant** screen and contains several important configurations and setups.

   Note that if your program will require more than one physical channel and your hardware is capable of supporting more than one channel at the same time, you must press and hold *Ctrl* and click simultaneously to choose multiple channels on the same task:

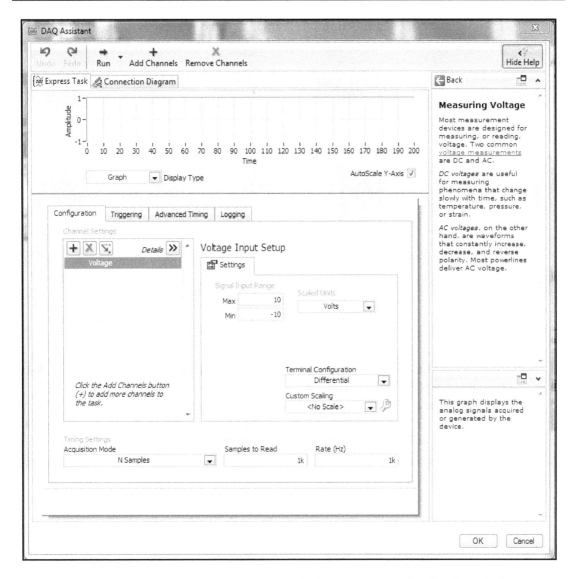

6. On top-left corner of the window, with the **Express Task** tab selected, there is **Run**, **Add Channels**, and **Remove Channels** option.

7. Once all other parameters are set, one may do a quick run and observe the resulting graph or table displayed. To see either one, choose **Display Type** from the pull-down menu.

8. If you click on the **Connection Diagram** tab, you can actually see a diagram of connected devices to the I/O pins:

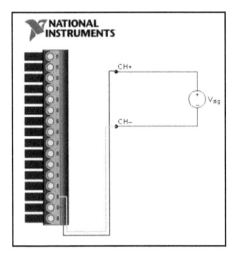

9. In the middle of the screen, there are four tabs; the **Configuration** tab is selected by default.

10. Note on the **Channel Settings**, **Voltage** appears, just as we selected it earlier for our measurement type.

11. Under **Voltage Input Setup**, we will enter –5 to 5 to be our desired range. This is to illustrate the point that we can choose our own limits; most devices will handle –10 to +10, which are the default values presented by LabVIEW.

12. From the pull-down menu **Terminal Configuration**, we will select **Differential** (the reader should properly understand grounding concepts).

13. Finally, we leave **<No Scale>** for **Custom Scaling**, which is the default value:

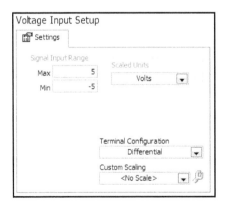

There are three very important choices under Timing Settings:

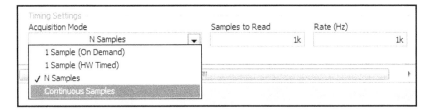

- From the **Acquisition Mode** pull-down menu, we may chooseN **Samples, 1 Sample (On Demand)** , **1 Sample (HW Timed)**, or **Continuous Samples**. Depending on the nature of data acquisition (and the hardware used), it is important to choose the right setting. For this example, we will use **N Samples** since we are also going to use a `while` loop to collect data continuously.
- The last two selections are very hardware-dependent. Hardware permitting, the resolution intended will determine the required settings for **Samples to Read** and **Rate (Hz)**. We will use **1k** for both settings in this example.

In most real-life cases, the data acquired needs to be saved for later use and analysis. There are at least two possible ways to log data as it is generated in LabVIEW. While using DAQ Assistant, the quicker way is to generate a log file from the same **DAQ Assistant** window:

1. Click on the **Logging** tab.
2. Place a checkmark next to **Enable TDMS Logging**.
3. Click on the folder icon to navigate to the desired location and name the file.
4. Note the **Logging Mode** choices available using the pull-down menu.
5. Change **Group Name** to a more specific and self-explanatory name if your program logic will require one.
6. Place a checkmark next to **Span multiple files** and select the file size. Otherwise, every time your program is executed, data will be appended to the original file.
7. When a VI with these settings is executed, two files are automatically generated: an Excel-importable TDMS file and another binary TDMS file which can be fed into another express VI (**Functions File I/O Read from Measurement File**).
8. Depending on the logic of a program (obviously not necessarily what the objective of this example is), the express VI Read From Measurement File can be used to read files created by its counterpart express VI Write Measurement File (located in the same pallet).

9. Click **OK** on the bottom-right of the DAQ Assistant:

DAQ Assistant will finalize the scripting and build the VI, and will place it on the **Block Diagram** window. Note all possible inputs on the left-hand side of the express VI. We will not add any specific inputs at this time, but the user may experiment with wiring some or all of the different possible inputs and compare the resulting triangular waveform generated.

Setting up of the DAQ assistant is now complete. Continue with the following steps to complete the Capture_Triangular_Wave VI:

1. Right-click on the **Front Panel** and place a **Waveform Graph** on the **Front Panel** window (**Controls | Modern | Graphs | Waveform Graph**).
2. On the **Block Diagram** window, wire the data output of the DAQ Assistant to the input of the Waveform Graph.
3. On the **Block Diagram**, place a while loop over **DAQ Assistant** and **Waveform Graph** (**Programming Structures While loop**).
4. Note that a **STOP** will appear on the bottom right of the while Loop. Move the cursor over the **STOP** icon until the arrow changes to a wire spool, right click and choose **Create Control**. Once the wiring is completed, a **STOP** button will also appear on the **Front Panel** window. To stop the program after execution has commenced, use this **STOP** button (and not the **STOP** button on the main LabVIEW toolbar) to terminate the running VI:

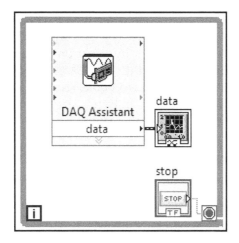

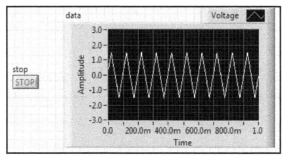

The `Capture_Triangular_Wave VI` is now complete. Run the VI and stop it after a few seconds. You should have **Front Panel** and **Block Diagram** windows similar to the preceding screenshots. Note that most of the data acquisition was done automatically by DAQ assistant.

Once the VI has stopped execution, navigate to the location where you saved the log files. If you have MS Excel installed on your computer, you should see a file with an icon similar to this:

As mentioned before, this file can be opened directly in Excel. Depending on the selected options, this file will have at least two books. The first one will contain header information only. Each time the VI executes, new header information is appended to this book and for each run, another new book is created (on the same Excel sheet) and numerical data is appended in the first row of the newly created book. This numerical data can be used to analyze the data and even graphed directly in Excel. The following graph is created using the results created by running the VI we just created:

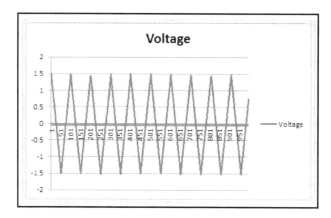

Summary

In this chapter, we used the automation capabilities of LabVIEW to create a VI that captures a triangular signal through simple DAQ hardware. We used the DAQ Assistant VI to do almost all of the required programming. Although assistant VIs are very easy to use and arrive at quick solutions, they lack the precise control capabilities that most real-life data acquisition conditions require. We will use NI-DAQmax data acquisition VIs in `Chapter 4`, *DAQ Programming Using LabVIEW*, to illustrate how LabVIEW can be used to measure a true physical phenomenon (such as temperature, light, and so on) and convert it to appropriate data that can be manipulated and analyzed with a computer.

4
DAQ Programming Using LabVIEW

In Chapter 3, *Using the DAQ Assistant to Automatically Generate LabVIEW Code*, we used an automated version of data acquisition. That was a quick and simple way for us to demo the power and some of the capabilities of LabVIEW. Needless to say, hardly any real-life situation is that simple and straightforward. In this chapter, we will formally define "data acquisition" and transform real-life phenomena such as voltage, light, temperature, and humidity, and transform the data such that it is understandable by a computer. In this chapter, we will use a Tektronix TDS 2022 scope and a Korad programmable power supply.

Definition of data acquisition

In the broadest context, data acquisition is the process of converting a real-life physical occurrence or phenomenon into computer-understandable data. **National Instruments** (refer to the official **NI** Certification Course Manual) breaks down this process into the following segments:

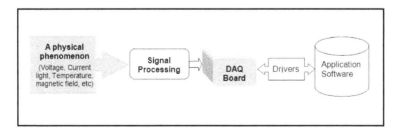

Capture signal generator waveforms

In Chapter 3, *Using the DAQ Assistant to Automatically Generate LabVIEW Code*, we generated a signal waveform and captured it through a USB DAQ. We used automation to accomplish this task. Although automation can be handy in many circumstances, the fact is, real-life data acquisition, especially in a more elaborate and complex environment, cannot possibly be available in preautomated form, and one must use standard LabVIEW functions and/or write customized functions from the ground up. In this chapter, we will use standard LabVIEW functions to acquire data and present it in human-understandable form. However, to establish a coherent comparison between what we did automatically (in other words, using express VIs) and how it might be done using standard functions (functions that are installed by LabVIEW) or custom functions (in other words, functions that are provided as drivers by a specific vendor) or those written by a LabVIEW programmer, we will redo the triangular signal capture example twice. Here are what the differences will be:

- In the first revised version, we will use regular LabVIEW functions (manual method) instead of utilizing DAQ Assistant as we did in the preceding chapter.
- In the second revision, we will use a Tektronix TDS 2022 (instead of USB DAQ 6008) and use functions (drivers) written specifically for Tektronix Oscilloscope.

In both cases, we will use a staircase signal instead of the triangular signal we used in the preceding chapter.

Staircase signal (USB DAQ version)

In this example, the hardware connection is exactly the same as it was in chapter 3. That is, we will directly connect the signal generator to USB DAQ 6008. We will use Analog Input 1. However, the Signal generator is set to generate a Staircase signal in this example.

Launch LabVIEW and start a new VI from the file menu and continue with the following steps:

1. Right click on the Block Diagram window and from Functions, select Measurement I/O, select NI-DAQmx and tack this pallet to the Block Diagram window. Now you can move this pallet to the appropriate location in your screen to make choosing and placing a Function on the Block Diagram and Front Panel windows with much ease and enhance the visibility of different windows. Note that when you move the mouse cursor on any Function icon, the complete name of the function is displayed. The same is true for each input and output of the any given function. Click on detail help, where available, to get further information about the function or data format and limitations of any input-output wire.

2. Click and drop the function Create Channel onto the Block Diagram window.

3. Right click on the Physical Channels input of the function and from the Create submenu, choose Constant. If you look under the drop-down menu arrow of the newly created constant, you will see all of the I/O channels that are available. The available channels, of course, are a function of the hardware connected to the PC. In our case, we have a USB DAQ 6008, so DAQ/ai0 to DAQ/ai7 are available. Recall that we have physically connected the function generator to ai0. Choose analog input 1.

4. Click and drop the function Timing onto the Block Diagram window. Make the following connections on this function:

    1. Connect the output wire Task Out of Virtual Channel to Task In of Timing.

    2. Connect the Error Out to Error In.

    3. Right click on the Sample mode of the timing function and from the submenu selection Create, choose control. Note that on the Front Panel window, a new selectable numeric ring is also created. Click on the up or down arrow to select Continuous Samples.

    4. Connect a constant value of 1000 to the Rate input of the DAQmx Timing.

5. Click and drop the Start function on the Block Diagram window. Connect both Task and Error wires.

6. Click and drop the "DAQmx Read" function on the Block Diagram window. Make sure the setting is changed to the following:

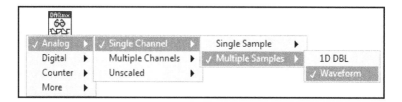

7. Connect a constant value of 1000 to the `number of samples` input of the DAQmx Read function.

8. Drop a **Waveform Graph** on the Front Panel window, and on the Block Diagram window, connect the "Data" output wire of the DAQmx Read to Waveform Graph.

9. Now, if you connect a **DAQmx Clear task** to the **DAQmx Read function**, you will have a working VI that will collect 1,000 samples and show it on the Front Panel window. Your circuit will look much like the following diagram, without the while loop and the accompanying stop. Save all and try to run the VI without the while loop. Later, add a while loop around the shown functions. Don't forget to add the Stop.

10. The completed Block Diagram should look similar to this:

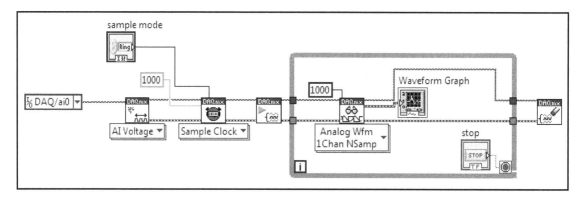

11. The completed VI should have a Front Panel similar to the following screenshot. Note that all objects on the Front Panel can be moved around and resized. The color and fonts can be changed and many other decorations may be applied to the Front Panel. Also note that all functions that we used are themselves made up of many other sub VIs. Open these VIs by double-clicking on them and explore what lies underneath each function.

12. Also change signal shape and amplitude and possibly other attributes of the signal on your function generator (these attributes vary substantially depending on the given function generator) and verify the specs with what LabVIEW displays:

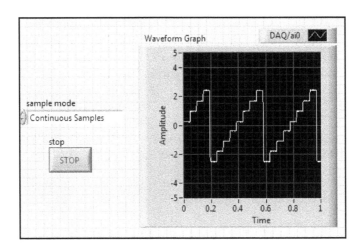

Staircase signal (Oscilloscope version)

We will attempt to duplicate the preceding example, this time using an oscilloscope. Here, we will be controlling an oscilloscope remotely. There should be little need to explain why it is necessary to be able to control an oscilloscope with LabVIEW. Aside from the actual various measurements that an oscilloscope can provide (beyond the scope of this book), it is essential to know how to connect to and use a given oscilloscope as one of the most important test and measurement instruments in use. When choosing an oscilloscope to automate and/or acquire data using LabVIEW, a few points are essential:

- Price
- Ability to be remotely controlled (Serial, Parallel, GPIB, Ethernet, and so on)
- Controlling protocol and driver software

Obviously, hardware products from National Instruments (NI) are most suitable for this purpose. But there are many occasions that certain required hardware is not available through NI. There are also other reasons that makes third-party equipment a more suitable choice (that is, price, regional support, military grade specs, and so on). Fortunately, not only do most industry leaders provide LabVIEW drivers with their equipment but also most of the not-so-well-known companies include LabVIEW drivers along with their hardware. Also, National Instruments provides a service that you may acquire LabVIEW drivers for a given instrument. Also note that at the heart of almost all device communications are SCPI commands and one should be able to write driver VIs based on SCPI commands with little effort.

The main purpose of this example is to learn how to use NI Max (part of the LabVIEW installation). With NI MAX, we will verify that all hardware is correctly recognized by LabVIEW and also learn how to install third-party LabVIEW drivers and use them in an example.

In this example, we use the following hardware:

- Tektronix TDS 2022 oscilloscope
- National Instruments GPIB-USB-HS
- FG085 miniDDS Function Generator

In this example, we have three essential pieces of hardware and primarily we need to take the necessary steps to establish proper connections between the devices and the LabVIEW computer. We will also (remotely) collect data from a precession test measurement equipment: a Tektronix TDS 2022 oscilloscope.

This particular oscilloscope has serial RS232 and GPIB for remote connection. We will use a GPIB to USB converter to connect the scope to the LabVIEW computer. To verify that we have the correct connection, connect the GPIB side of the converter to the scope and USB side to the computer. The NI GPIB-USB converter also has a driver, Assuming you have installed the driver for the converter, we will fire up NI MAX (look for its icon on your desktop; it should have been installed when LabVIEW was installed on the computer). You should be able to find both devices on the left pane of the window once NI MAX is launched. If you look closely, you will see the three devices that are connected to the computer.

If you expand all nested arrows, you will see all connected devices. In our example, under GPIB-USB-HS, you will see TDS 2022 Scope is connected to the GPIB to USB converter:

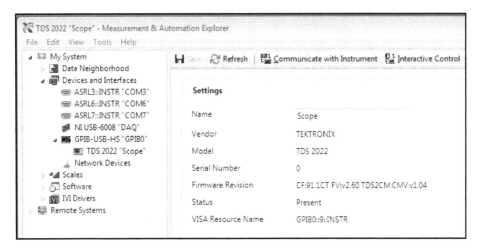

On the right side of the window, there are two menu items that when clicked on will launch two very useful applications. The menu items are self-explanatory of what each application does. In the **Send String** window, any SCPI command may be entered and the response from the device is displayed in **String Received**. To verify that we have proper communication with the oscilloscope through the GPIB-USB converter, we will use the very standard SCPI command (*IDN):

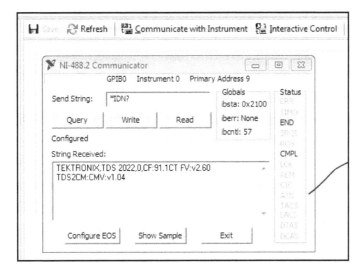

To do so, type `*IDN?` and press the **Query** button. If all drivers are installed properly, you see that Tektronix TDS 2022 will return `TEKTRONIX,TDS 2022,0,CF:91.1CT FV:v2.60 TDS2CM:CMV:v1.04`. This indicates that all is well and we can start to utilize the scope.

Oscilloscope functions in LabVIEW function pallets

Next, we need to make sure that software drivers are correctly installed in LabVIEW for the correct model of the instrument we have: the oscilloscope. Some vendors provide the software in the box with the hardware sold. Otherwise, a little search on the NI site will do the job. Usually, there are two flavors of the drivers for these devices: "Plug and Play" as well as "Plug and play (project style)". Complete and detailed installation is also available on the NI site. Note the path and two versions of the drivers installed. This is for demo and installation of both versions, while perfectly OK but not necessary useful. Note that if you are planning on making an application with an installer out of your VI(s), all drivers and non LabVIEW standard functions need to be included in the process of creating an installer for the application:

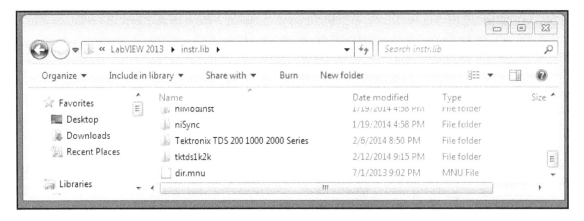

Once the software has installed properly, it will appear on your functions plug when you click on the Block Diagram window. For example, a device such as an oscilloscope will appear like this:

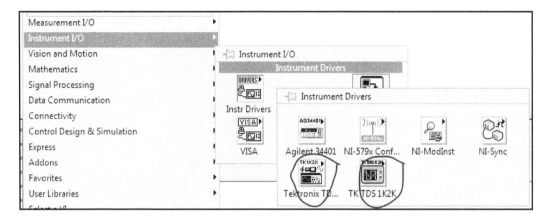

The following VI is right off of the example provided by the drivers provided by the NI LabVIEW. Double-click on any of the VIs until you reach where you can see all SCPI commands. Once the VI starts running, LabVIEW takes over the control of the scope and on many instruments, local buttons cease to function while the instrument is being remotely controlled:

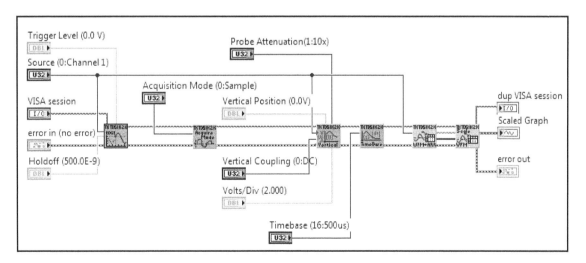

The VI with the preceding Block Diagram creates a more detailed and much more controls and indicators but for the sake of comparison of the two waveforms on the LabVIEW screen and oscilloscope screen, in the left just waveform part of the output is shown. In the right, we have a picture of the oscilloscope see next two pictures side by side.

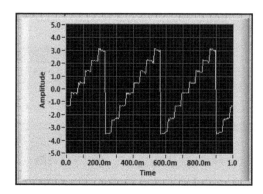

The preceding signal capture is from LabVIEW; the following figure comes from the oscilloscope:

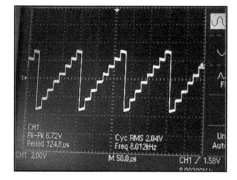

Stepping through voltages

In this example, we will use a programmable power supply to step through five different voltages (since we use an array, the number of voltages can be as many as the number of array elements). We will send SCPI commands to a programmable power supply (KORAD KA3005P programmable DC power supply) to set the voltage. In the next step, we query the instrument to report back the value that the power supply is currently set on. Finally, we will collect all the returned values in a different array.

The power supply is connected to the LabVIEW computer via USB. We will use serial communication to send commands and collect returned values. The communication part of the VI is achieved via a SUB VI called Serial P.P.S.

To achieve the prceding scenario, we will only need four SCPI commands:

1. OUT1: This will set the output to ON mode
2. VSET1: This will set the output channel 1 to <value> volts
3. VSET1 : This will query voltage at channel 1
4. OUT0: This will turn the output off

Note that the SCPI commands used in this particular programmable power supply are very simple. In general, SCPI commands can be, and usually are, longer and much more complex:

```
MEASUrement:IMMed:VALue?
```

Let's start with the SUB VI Serial programmable power supply or Serial P.P.S. As mentioned here, we need to send SCPI commands to the power supply and return the response of the power supply. This SUB VI facilitates the read-write that is repeated several times and it also makes the code much readable and manageable.

Create serial Read-Write sub VI

To create a sub VI, follow these steps:

1. Right click on Block Diagram and from Instrument I/O choose the VISA pallet.
2. From the VISA pallet:
    1. Place a "VISA Configure serial port".
    2. Connect a "Control" to the input.
    3. Default baud rate is 9600 and you may connect a constant to it, or just leave it to use the default value.
    4. Place a "VISA write" and connect the serial reference wire and error wires.
    5. Add a control to the input wire of the "VISA write".
    6. Place a variable control delay (use Functions Programming Structures Flat sequence).
    7. Place a "VISA Property Node" and connect the serial reference line. Right click on the property node and choose "Bytes at Port".

8. Place a "Read Visa" and connect the input and output wires as diagram here:

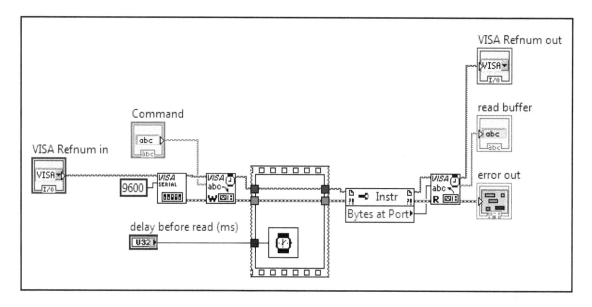

3. Finally, create a SUB VI.

Power supply voltage steps

What this VI attempts to do is simply set five different voltages and query the current value every time that a new value is set. We also need to set the output of the power supply to ON mode in the beginning and set it to OFF at the end. We are going to use an array to send SCPI commands to achieve each step.

We begin by creating this unpopulated array:

1. Place an "Array constant" on the Block Diagram: Functions | Programming | Array | array Constant.
2. Drop a "String Constant" on the "Array Constant": Functions | Programming | String | String Constant.
3. Fill the array element as shown in the VI. The array should have 12 elements:

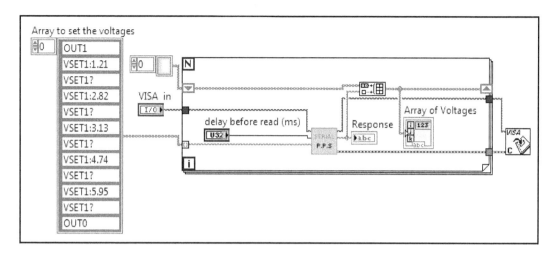

4. Add a "For Loop": Functions Programming Structures "For Loop".
5. Drop the SUB VI we built inside the "For Loop": Functions Select a VI… navigate, and find the SUBVI and place it inside the "For Loop".
6. Place a "Build Array" inside the loop. Click on "Build Array" and expand it to two inputs.
7. Connect the "Read buffer" output of the SUB VI and connect it to the "element" of the build array. Connect the "Appended array" side of the "Build Array" to the right edge of the for loop. Right click on the connection point and from the available menu, choose "Replace with Shift Register". The cursor changes to a down arrow. Click on the left side of the "For Loop".
8. Finish the VI by connecting the rest of the wiring and adding the proper input and output indicators.
9. Do not forget to close VISA outside of the "For Loop".
10. Note that the "For Loop" does not need an index constant. The iteration number of the "'For loop" would be automatically set to the number of array elements.
11. To run the VI, the correct COM port must be selected. Look in Device Manager (under Windows). This particular one would appear as "Nuvoton Virtual Com Port(COM X)".

12. When you run this VI, you will see what appears in "String Indicator" called "Response" and then the VI will populate the "array of Voltages":

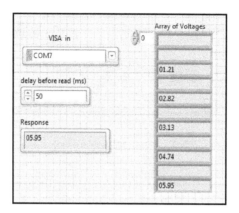

Verify Data Acquired

As you will most likely notice, there are empty array elements in the output array on the Front Panel of this VI. See the previous array. There are very fundamental reasons I have left the VI as is (that is, if the purpose of the VI is to collect voltages, obviously we are not interested in blank array elements). Fundamental to data acquisition is verification of the data acquired in clearly defined milestones. Here we use "milestone" in the broadest sense of the word. A milestone may be the values a SUB VI is programmed to do or how a complete product is designed to function. Usually, a product is the end result of the labor of different teams of engineers working in collaboration. What may be considered the end of a working product (or part of a product) for a team of developers often is not where the collaborating team may be able to directly start to resume further development. A temperature sensor may send actual temperature values in string form, then again many temperature sensors only send analog values, only representing values based on increase in resistance, due to ambient temperature changes. One may somewhat correctly argue that the concept explained before is true in every segment of the industry or obvious or even elementally but the fact of the matter is that in data acquisition, examination of data in a particular shape or form that may be represented is detrimentally important. For example, as SCPI is the most prevalent communication command in test and measurement instruments, is more than one may expect different than TL1(Transaction Language 1) widely used in telecommunications; although in both cases a series of strings are sent to a machine and a response is retrieved in the same general concept that SCPI operates.

Power Supply Voltage Steps: Revision 1

In this revision of the Power Supply Voltage Steps example, we will accomplish three tasks:

- We will create a SUB VI to collect voltages from an oscilloscope
- We will add condition selections such that the blank array elements are removed
- We will add code to display measured voltage as opposed to set voltages

To create a SUB VI that will use the oscilloscope to display the measured voltages that the power supply puts out, we will do the following:

1. From the Tektronix functions pallet, choose and place "Initialize.vi" and "Read Measurement.vi" on a Block Diagram of a new VI.
2. Connect a Boolean False to the "Reset" input of the Initialize.vi.
3. Connect serial input and output VISA as in the following diagram.
4. Right click on the "Measurement Type" input of the measurement type VI and choose "Mean" from the drop-down menu.
5. Create a SUB VI and save all:

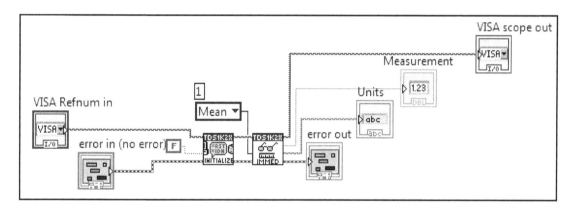

With this SUB VI in place, we can modify the original VI to implement parts 2 and 3.

There are four main changes needed, as enumerated with text comments in the Block Diagram:

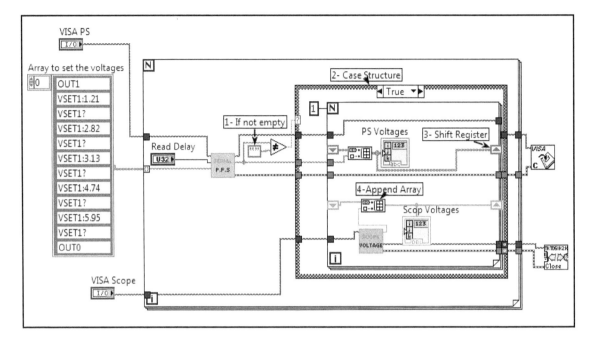

1. We will add a compare for empty string.
2. If the string is not empty, the "Case Structure" will switch to "True" case and the data is captured in two arrays.
3. We will use "Build Array" from the Array pallet from the Programming function and connect the input string to the "element" input side and connect the output array side to the right edge of the "for loop".
4. Right click on the right edge where the array wire is connected to the "For Loop" and from the menu, click "Shift Register" and click on the left edge of the "For Loop" and connect the wire from array input of the to the down array on the left edge of the for loop.

5. Place the SUB VI "Scope Voltage" inside of the "For loop" and repeat creating a Build array similar to step 4:

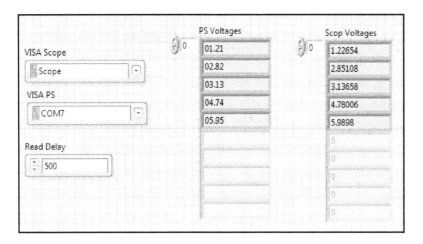

The Front Panel of the VI should look like the preceding screenshot. Note a couple of important points related to data acquisition and LabVIEW:

- The way we have programmed this VI, we collect the data in two different arrays but every time the VI is run, the data collected is appended to both arrays created.

- The number of significant figures returned is dependent on both default values set on LabVIEW and the instruments the data is acquired from. Note the current numbers in two arrays we have created. A meaningful calculation of, for example, the percent difference calculation of the value we set the voltage value and measured value must take into consideration how accurate each instrument is.

- The last thing to consider in this example is how fast the loops can run and how long each instrument is able to stabilize and return the answer. Note that there is a "read delay" input in this example. Change the value and note the response from each instrument. Since we use serial communication, when the there is a threshold beyond which this power supply does not stabilize fast enough and incorrect values are returned.

Summary

In this chapter, we started by defining what precisely the definition of data acquisition is. Further, we went through programs that actually used a programmable power supply and an oscilloscope where we set the power supply to specific values and measured the true output value of the power supply via an oscilloscope.

In the next chapter, we begin with debugging issues.

5

Debugging Techniques

Even if you are a very experienced programmer and a seasoned engineer, chances are that you will make mistakes while coding and will need help to resolve all occurring warnings and errors to complete your program. We all know that one may open a text editor and write some code and have a running operating system compile the code. But serious collaborative programming requires a professional IDE. Visual Studio (as an example) jumps to my mind as I write these lines. It seems every day a new language appears in the industry and along with it a new development environment.

As a comparison, LabVIEW has gone one step beyond others since its inception, which is its ability to communicate seamlessly with hardware. LabVIEW has a very comprehensive and reliable IDE that is very intelligent such that the intelligence built in LabVIEW may be mistaken as "anybody can program in LabVIEW", it is "trivial" such that they do not need to go through formal training to use it professionally. This is not true. Although I am strongly pro formal education, but in my long career as a LabVIEW developer I have met many people who are self-taught LabVIEW professionals only in one or more area of the LabVIEW. In this chapter, we will go through some areas that a developer needs to keep an eye on.

Observing syntax errors in LabVIEW (as opposed to most other IDEs) is much more obvious and practically instantaneous to each function that is added to either development window. In most modern IDEs, there are many features that help programmers to complete code or auto indent (text-based languages) and many other so-called "bells and whistles" that are often needed and some are absolutely necessary!! LabVIEW by nature is "smarter" than most (if not all) other programming environments. This holds true also when debugging time arrives.

As we mentioned in Chapter 1, *LabVIEW Basics*, LabVIEW opens two windows simultaneously once it is launched: a Block Diagram and a Front Panel window. These windows have both menu items and a strip of quick access tools that change shape depending on the specific stage of development one may be in. With little effort, you may see that these buttons react to a given condition (and some change shape) as you progress through the development stages. The emphasis of this chapter is on detecting sources of errors and understanding the debugging techniques in LabVIEW. With a little experimentation, you will have a realistic notion of what the changes in shapes of these buttons indicate. One fundamental difference between LabVIEW and other IDEs (especially with text-based programming environments) is that in LabVIEW, since functions are connected to each other through data carrying wires, you may quickly run into a situation where you must resolve the current error. That is, before you can place the next function on any of the windows and be able to wire it. The following figure shows a collection of some of the buttons in various stages:

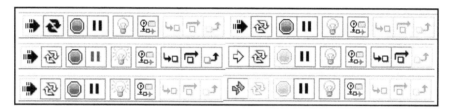

At first glance, the preceding figure seems confusing or even intimidating. But in reality, working with these buttons is simpler than what the preceding figure may suggest. In fact, the preceding figure is constructed from six different common situations, which are carefully placed next to each other only to make a quick comparison easier and possible. In fact, only the very first button, the "Run" button changes to four shapes and the rest are indicating either an ON or OFF state. As always, practice will help sort things out much better.

Error conditions

The most common and most obvious error condition is when an attempt is made to wire (connect) two incompatible objects (different types) or functions together. In this condition a broken wire appears. A VI with even one broken wire will not run. Most functions have an error input and output that are very helpful. Error wires are a cluster and carry more than one form of information. Note the expanded Front Panel window showing the three components (Status, Code, and Source) that are encompassed in an error cluster notice. In the following figure (left) a hypothetical VI that does nothing; therefore, there is no error, so the status is a green checkmark (this is a Boolean value) and can be used as such.

A useful and common use for this Boolean value is to use the false state (where there is no error) to continue running with the rest of the program where you suspect the possibility of a frequent error condition that may exist. In our example, note that we start by opening a serial port; this is a common source of error and one should check for a proper serial condition before continuing. For simplicity and the main interest of this chapter (error conditions), we have deliberately omitted this step. One improvement to the example we show in this chapter is to enclose the for-loop inside a "case structure" where we check to make sure that we have successfully opened a serial port before we continue. On the left side of the following figure, we show an (induced) error condition where the VI fails to open a serial port. Here "status" indicates the error condition. The "code" window shows an error number (that may be generic LabVIEW numbers) or programmed specifically to be specific to an instrument or a VI. Finally, "source" is a string that explains the error code. Note that not all functions have error checking embedded in them. For example, simple mathematics is done without using error in and out. But one of the very handy uses of having error in and out to our VIs and SUB-VIs is to use error wires to enforce a desired order of execution:

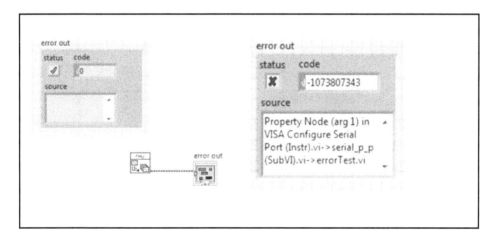

There are a couple of cases that may be considered as exceptions to this rule:

1. You may place some functions on either window (Block Diagram or Front Panel) and NOT connect any wires (there may be other functions that are connected and working or NOT!!), but LabVIEW will not "complain" and you will not get a broken wire. But there are functions that demand a minimal number of input(s) and/or output(s) The following example will run perfectly fine (make sure you run it in continuous run mode). The tool bar will look similar to the top part of the following figure:

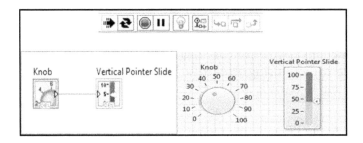

2. Now we add several functions that (still) do not break the VI (do not cause a broken wire) and the VI will continue to execute:

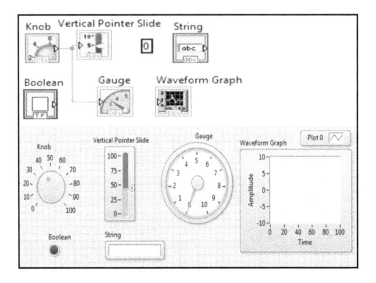

The VI will still function and all extra functions are accepted.

3. Now try to connect the "Boolean" to the Waveform Graph, you will immediately get a broken arrow on the "Run" button and the VI will no longer be executable. Your "Run" button will look as follows:

4. It is very obvious why you got a broken arrow (in step 4,) and of course how to fix it. But in reality, a broken arrow due to a simple mismatch or unconnected wire (to a required input of a function or SUB VI) often occurs after you have worked on a program that has many VIs and SUB-VIs that collectively have been working fine up to that moment. At such times, a fix is not so simple. As we continue with debugging techniques, we will explore ways to debug and fix errors and warnings.

Debugging – broken arrow

As mentioned previously, when a VI is "seriously!" broken, it does not run and a broken arrow is displayed. Since the error is immediately recognized by LabVIEW, usually in such particular cases, the fix is probably simple (unless a major design error is recognized). A more difficult situation maybe where there are no obvious errors, but the VI does not do what we intend it to do. We will now take a closer look at a version of a VI we used in Chapter 4, *DAQ Programming Using LabVIEW*:

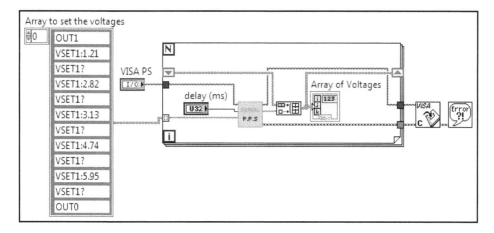

When we run the preceding VI several times, we will notice a couple of issues with the VI. Note that a displayed array may be extended horizontally or vertically:

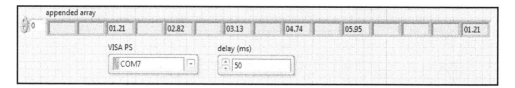

- The array gets longer and longer and new values are appended to the end of the results from the previous run
- There are blank array elements between the array entries (this was an error with the logic of the VI and we fixed it by adding a check for blank array elements)

To fix the issue, we know that we need to initialize the array before each run. That is, the array needs to start empty every time it is executed. To do so, we create an empty array and append it to the "array of voltages." To do so, we:

1. Drop a Functions|array |"array constant" on the Block Diagram window.
2. Drop a Functions | Numeric | "DBL Numeric Constant" on the block diagram. Drag and drop a Numeric constant onto the array constant. Now we have an array of doubles. You may have caught the arising issue already. Once we connect the empty constant arrow to the input shift register wire, we immediately get a broken wires error. The block diagram will look similar to the following Block Diagram. We have successfully induced an error. We have created a type mismatch and obviously a broken wire. Note the colored arrows:

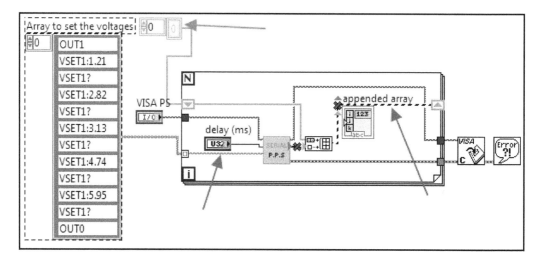

Recall that we created an array of Doubles (Green arrow.) But we needed an array String (red arrow) since the input array of SCPI commands are lines of string that we intend to send to programmable voltage supply. Finally, note the blue arrow that points to the broken arrow. When you run this VI, LabVIEW will present you with a dialogue box that lists all the errors and warnings. You can click on each item on the list of errors and click on the "Show Error" button and LabVIEW will highlight the specific error selected. The following screenshot shows the current errors on this VI. To fix the VI, all we need to do is to make sure that the initialization array has the same type (string) as the returned values by the SUB-VI and appended array that displays the final array. Therefore, change step 2 to Drop a Functions Numeric "String Constant".

Debugging – highlight execution

Given the nature of data transfer used in LabVIEW (wires) one of the most useful debugging tools available in LabVIEW is the concept of "Highlighted Execution".

If you click on the light bulb, LabVIEW will slow down the execution of VI, and one or several moving dots will trace the order of execution and transfer of data will be visible and traceable by the programmer. Also, in this state, all the VI starts off dimmed and as the execution continues, the parts of code that are executed exit the dimmed state. Another very important tidbit to notice is that in "Highlight Execution" while the dots travel on the wires that are currently being executed, the actual value that is carried at the moment on that wire is also displayed. The following figure is a partial cropped part of an example code of one of the examples that are shipped with LabVIEW.

Note: the left side of the picture is executed while the right side, where a loop is about to complete execution, is still dimmed and it will stay dimmed until at least one iteration of the loop is completed. Also note that on all executed wires, the current value of the wire(or the segment) is displayed. Finally, note the various distinctly colored dots on the lines (some are pointed out with the colors associated with each wire):

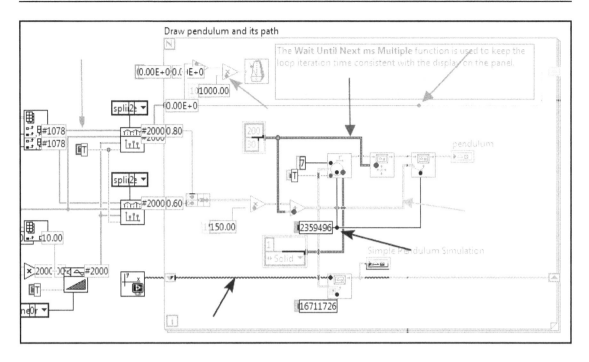

Draw pendulum and its path

Debugging – Set Breakpoint

As the title suggests, a programmer may set one or several breakpoints on various wires on different locations of a given VI. As expected, once the execution of the VI reaches the given stop point, LabVIEW stops the execution of the VI and waits for the user input.

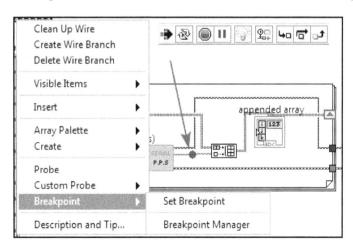

As indicated in the preceding figure, to create a Breakpoint in a given location, right-click on the exact spot where you want to have a breakpoint, and from the sub menu belonging to the **Breakpoint** select **Set Breakpoint**. Note that the preceding screenshot is a composite diagram that shows the tool bar section of the Block Diagram window of the same example we have been using in this chapter. We have placed a breakpoint right after the SUB-VI and just before a value is added to the array. Note also that in this particular case, we have also enabled Highlight Execution. Currently, all tools are simultaneously available to us. From left to right:

1. Of course the **Run** button is pressed and the VI is running. Note that if our VI did not have a loop, we could have use **Continuous Run** adjacent to the right of the **Run** button.

2. Knowing that we may press the "Stop" button at anytime (for obvious reasons, we will skip the explanation as to what the stop button does), but one very, very important point it is necessary to make here is that in an example such as the one we are using in this chapter, note that we open a serial port connection just prior to entering the loop. We also have a closed serial port just after the for loop. It is vital that we *properly* close the serial port(s) and/or any other types of ports (that is, GPIB, USB, and so on) we have opened. Stopping a VI with the "Stop" button from the tool bar menu will abruptly stop the execution of the LabVIEW program while physically our instruments are not aware that the program is no longer running and the state of a port that has not been closed properly most likely is *unknown*. While it is impossible to know what an instrument does in an unknown state, on many instruments the serial port stays open until an overflow occurs thus requiring some form of (including a hard) reset. Since the port was not closed properly, depending on the instrument and the specific operating system used, often the port stays open and if a program that has improperly stopped execution attempts to restart, the open port in the beginning of the program encounters (a false in-use port) and LabVIEW indicates a (false) error such as the port is already open. Another reaction of an operating system may be to simply remove the ports from its stack and indicate non-existing port(s), which require a hardware reset. In data acquisition systems (where usually there is more than one hardware connected to the computer running the LabVIEW), hardware resetting instruments is neither easy to handle nor proper.

3. Once the program reaches the first breakpoint it stops, and the Pause/Continue button, along with the last three buttons, Step Into, Step Over, and Step Out become available. These buttons behave (intelligently) differently depending on what the entire VI consists of and where one might use the breakpoint(s.) In the example, we are using:
   1. Step Into : Will step to the next iteration.
   2. Step Over: Will also step to the next iteration.
   3. Step Out : Will finish the for loop.
4. Every time one of the Step buttons is pressed, LabVIEW continues to the next appropriate step and draws a blinking or rotating dashed line around the covered area. Note that using these debugging steps may also open a SUB-VI (if existing or possible) and you may step through the function within a SUB-VI.

Once again, note that these debugging tools stop the LabVIEW application only, and the hardware attached to this VI may and probably will continue to function, unaware that the actual software running it is stopped. In most cases, the hardware may simply overflow the port and disconnect or some form of timeout may occur. But consider an actual common situation where a high voltage high current power board is under development, test, or automation. These boards are commonly designed to withstand much higher than normal-use spikes in voltage and current draw. But suppose you set a breakpoint after a segment of code that sets up very high voltage or much higher current draw that in reality a spike is meant to last (spikes in order of nano or milliseconds.) But your code stops for minutes or longer. The result of this situation is dangerous and it sometimes results in serious hardware failure. As the emphasis of this book is data collection through hardware, one must be aware of situations like this much more than a programmer who is programming "software" only.

Debugging – Probe, Custom Probe

As mentioned earlier, LabVIEW objects and functions are connected to each other through data carrying wire. One of the very effective methods of debugging is to create probes and custom probes in various locations, on wires of interests. Probes or (custom probes) in conjunction with highlighted execution or breakpoints in place, LabVIEW will open a new window (right bottom on the following diagram) that concurrently shows the value of each wire where each probe has been placed. To create a probe (or a custom probe), right-click on the specific locations where you want a probe to be placed and select **Probe** or **Custom Probe**.

This example simply consists of three random number generators that are connected to each other to do arbitrary simple mathematical manipulations. We have enclosed the connection inside a while loop and placed a 1000 milliseconds delay inside the while loop to slow down the loop so that an observer can distinguish between the numbers that are continuously generated. A Boolean indicator is connected to the final value that blinks every time the final value is greater than 10. While the VI is running, click on each of the break points and observe its current value:

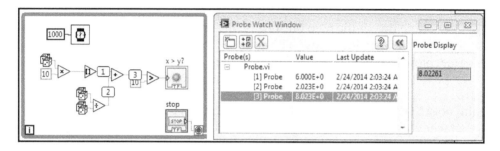

Summary

In this chapter, we have explored most, but not all debugging techniques that LabVIEW provides. Error cluster, broken wires, set breakpoints, and set probes are among the most widely used tools and techniques used to debug a VI. Special cautionary notes were included in this chapter to remind us that debugging techniques require slowing down the process, or abruptly stopping a running VI. This is because as our emphasis is on data acquisition, which requires direct connection and control of the hardware and instruments, special care must be taken to note what immediate effect debugging might have on connected hardware and instruments.

Special cautionary notes were included in this chapter to highlight data acquisition special environment development in which we are dealing with both a running software and one or more hardware. Debugging in this situation takes on a whole new meaning in regards to some of the equipment used. One must take special note that slowing down software may or may not slow down the associated hardware. The same goes for a "hang" or a "freeze". That is, the software may hang while the hardware is still running, or while the hardware may have stopped responding, but the software may be in an oblivious state in reference to the hardware. As an example, imagine the case in which that software is set to increase the voltage incrementally. Also imagine that for reasons unforeseen or due to erroneous logic, the software (freezes or hangs) just simply jumps to the next section of the code without properly limiting the voltage increase. Continuous voltage increase may have disastrous results.

6
Real-World DAQ Programming Techniques

We are almost halfway through the book and we have mostly talked about real-world phenomena and how we are able to use a series of VIs to quantify and represent a given real-life phenomenon (such as temperature, voltage/current movement, and so on) and classify and quantify them with numbers or values understandable to a computer. In doing so, we have been concentrated on getting one action done, but have ignored the *real* thinking processes and methods required just prior to running that certain VI and all work that must be done after running our main VI, when the objective of a program is a complete working system.

In other words, what we have done so far here is *prove the concept*. While in real-life conditions, a system (consisting of both software and hardware must stand on its own merits and results), and inputs and outputs of it must be repeatable, documentable, and generally understandable by a peer or a colleague. Even what we are working on now may be targeted for production where very minimum ID is desired.

In Chapter 7, *Real-Time Issues*, rather than a lab condition, we will focus on minimal techniques that target a factory or a production environment.

When a system (software-hardware) must be used then:

- A real GUI almost always becomes necessary; a simple front panel of a VI will not suffice any longer
- Input data must come from a separate file and it cannot be hardcoded
- Initialization of ports, hardware, and so on, needs to be taken care of in the beginning of the software, and an appropriate message must be presented to the operator

- Software needs to recover from the initialization error, port polling and device renunciation, and assignment for a set amount of time before presenting the operator with the option to check connections, continue, or stop
- Stop, in most cases, brings down devices that require linear bringing up and shutting down

Depending on the task presented to the developer, there are four scenarios that are commonly used in real-life DAQ programming techniques:

- Using event manager
- Using State Machines
- Production-ready software-minimum sections
- May not need advanced functions

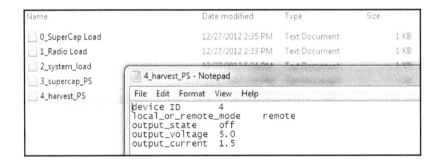

Using event manager

Event managers are triggered by external events; depending on the event triggered they do one or several tasks. Usually, the tests are limited in size while the operator is required for the duration of the task.

Installing LINX

The installation of LINX (http://sine.ni.com/nips/cds/view/p/lang/en/nid/212478) is a much improved path to support embedded platforms such as Arduino, ChipKit, and even National Instrument's own myRIO. Once LINX is downloaded and installed onto LabVIEW, under the main menu item **Tools**, submenu items, similar to the following screenshot, will be visible. Using **LINX Firmware Wizard...** will present developers with simple and easy to follow instructions to complete firmware installation.

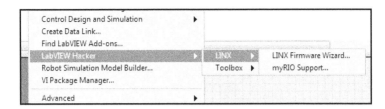

Note that the LabVIEW function pallet for Arduino must be installed, just like any other tools package using **JKI VI Package Manager** before one can take full advantage of this platform.

The following image on the left depicts the first screen with multiple drop-down menus that guide the user to install the required firmware. Note the drop-down menus from which one can select **Device Family**, **Device Type**, and **Firmware Program Interface**.

The screenshot on the right illustrates the LINX top-level function pallet:

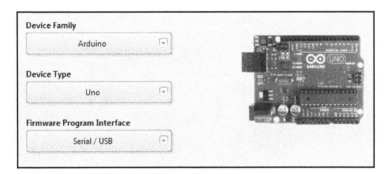

Acquiring distance measurements using Parallax USR with an Arduino

Acquiring the precise distance to or from an object is entrenched in so many devices we use these days that we often wonder how people used to live without them just a few years ago. From every cell phone that we use, to driverless cars that are now coming to streets, measuring proximity to a nearby object plays a pivotal role in engineering and data acquisition. A robot vacuum cleaner traverses living rooms and bedrooms avoiding objects while cleaning carpets and floors. Modern TVs understand and respond to hand gestures. Defining and recording the exact position of an object in space and its position relative to its neighboring objects has evolved very rapidly.

Even laser gun slinging exploding robots in movies need to measure distance to an object and move accordingly. Not all of that is Computer Generated Graphics. Acquiring the precise distance to an object ranges from a very simple number to extremely complicated GPS and devices that control directions, positions, and movements at the same time. In this example, we will use a PING ultrasonic sensor (http://www.parallax.com) connected to an Arduino Uno to acquire accurate (relatively speaking depending on the range and accuracy of a device) distances to nearby object(s). This device only uses one I/O pin. By measuring the returned time (echo) of a burst of Ultrasonic pulse, this device outputs distance measurements. The device only uses three pins.

Connections

- Connect pin labeled "SIG" to digital I/O pin 7
- Connect pin labeled "5V" to 5 volts output of an Arduino board
- Connect pin labeled "GND" to one of the two pins labeled ground on the Arduino board
- Arduino is connected to a PC through the available USB connection

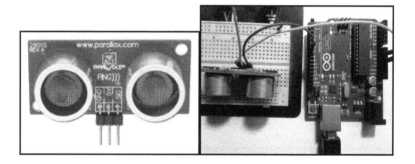

LabVIEW Program – serial communication through USB

The structure behind coding is simple and always the same when using an Arduino. Although TCP communication is also available, we use serial through USB and open a communication port to the computer. Then the code enters a loop and collects data while in the loop. The *stop* button will exit the loop and we will perform one very important last step when dealing with communications through the serial port, which is to close all opened ports appropriately.

Before any coding may commence, on a Windows machine traverse to the device manager and verify that all drivers are in place and that Arduino is assigned to a specific port. Note the port number.

Block diagram

1. Open a new VI and save it with an appropriate name.
2. Open the LINX function platter and place the "initialize" VI on the Block Diagram window.
3. The com port on your system may not be the same as the one on this VI. Verify your port assigned to Arduino from your control panel settings.
4. Right-click and connect three controls for serial connection, Platform, and interface and choose as marked on the arrow "Opening serial port".
5. Place a while loop and drop a "Ping.vi".
6. Drag and drop the three indicators.
7. Wire all connections as in the following block diagram:

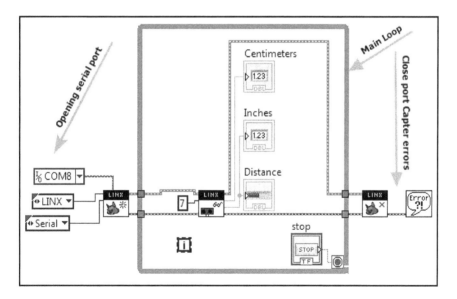

Front Panel

Your Front Panel should look similar to the following screenshot:

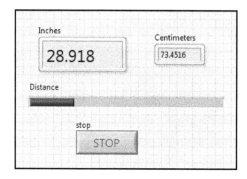

Click Run and place an object in front of the PING ultrasonic. You should see the distance measured in centimeters and inches; also the blue bar will show you a relative length based on the setting you choose. Move the object closer to; or away from the sensor and notice the dynamic measurement and display of the distance, accordingly.

Duty cycle and PWM

Pulse-Width Modulation, or PWM, basically creates a pseudo analog voltage. In reality, PWM is a square wave where the percentage of the time where the signal is up versus the time the signal is down, called the duty cycle is varied, therefore and in effect one would get a variable voltage. In the following example, we will create a variable duty cycle; using the PWM capabilities of an Arduino compatible device called Uno32. This board is officially called "**chipKIT Uno32 Prototyping Platform**" and it is based on Microchip® PIC32MX320F128 and an original Arduino development environment. National Instrument is the parent company of Digilent®, the original manufacturer of this board. The board runs at 80 Mhz, but it has a 32 bit MIPS processor. As mentioned previously, the real signal produced is a square wave and to see the actual waveform we will connect the output to an oscilloscope.

Connections

Note that the Uno32 is Arduino-compatible; as such it must have proper firmware installed:

- Connect the board to a PC via a USB -> mini B
- Install LINX (see the Installing LINX section)

- Connect pin 5 to the oscilloscope output (yellow wire in the image) and pin labeled GND to scope ground (blue wire in the image)
- You may need to adjust the scope to capture the proper signal
- Note the value at 2.53 V at the bottom of the screen on the image on the right

The left image depicts an Uno32 and with a wiring connection to the scope:

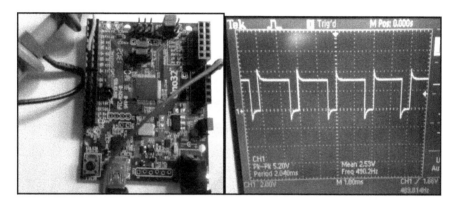

LabVIEW, LINX Duty Cycle Control

Block diagram

1. Open a new VI and save it with an appropriate name.
2. Open the LINX function platter and place "initialize" VI on the Block Diagram window.
3. Similar to the previous example, add a serial port selector and platform selector to the "Initialize" VI from the LINX function platter.
4. Create a while loop, drop a "Set Duty Cycle" from the LINX function platter, drop a "Wait" from the Timing pallet, and connect a small wait to it (100ms). The "Wait" is for a good programming habit and it is not fundamental to this particular program, given that there is only one VI (and various subVIs). Without a "Wait," a while loop may lock a processor in some computers.
5. On the Front Panel window, drop a "Dial" from the Numeric panel.
6. Connect pin 5 to the PWM selector of "Set Duty Cycle" VI. Note that this pin is selected for this particular board and there are many other boards on the market. Refer to the documentation for the exact or compatible board you may use.
7. Close the port outside the loop as in the previous example.

8. Connect all wires as in the following diagram.
9. Verify that "Set Duty Cycle 1 Chan" is selected.

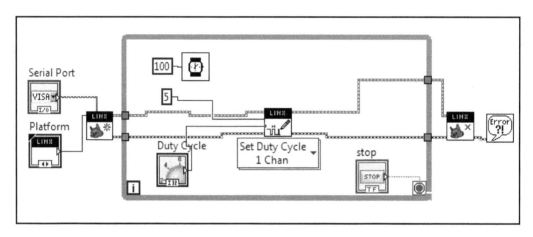

Front Panel

1. On the From Panel, verify that LINX is selected as the platform and that the Serial Port number matches the port number as indicated by the computer and the operating system you use.
2. Set the Duty Cycle from 0 to 255:

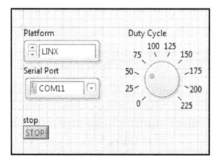

Start running the program and use your mouse to vary the Duty Cycle and note the change in signal shape and mean value of the voltage. The following two images capture the scope screen at 50 and 200. A zero represents a duty cycle of 0% and 255 represents a 100% duty cycle.

See DutyCycle at (`www.Put_Location_URL`).

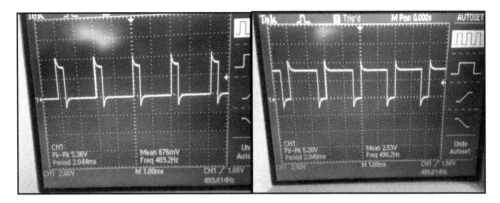

Simultaneous data acquisition – NI DAQ and the Arduino Uno

Data acquisition is in fact meaningless without the proper interpretation of acquired data. As stated at the beginning of this book, data acquisition consists of converting a real-life phenomenon into computer-understandable and human-interpretable data. When we acquire a temperature using a sensor and a DAQ, at one point or another we are converting a voltage (or a current value) into a temperature as adegree. In this process, a sensor that is calibrated within a given specification and accuracy range is connected to a DAQ, which in turn converts the received data (as an input) and communicates the output to a software that ultimately presents it in a human-understandable form; not to oversee the accuracy of the DAQ and the software representation.

What we do in real life is measure the accuracy of a sensor, a measuring device, or a DAQ in our system against another one, that we have more data for and trust more.

In the following example, we will combine and at the same time compare the data we acquired using LabVIEW, a National Instrument DAQ, and an Arduino, as well as human visuals (recorded in a clip!) with the use of a much more accurate FLUKE 117.

In the following example, we will connect:

1. A USB Programmable DC power supply.
2. A FLUKE 117.
3. A National Instrument NI USB 6008.
4. An Arduino Uno rev3.

We will use a breadboard (ideally a short soldered connection or even a PCB should be used) to connect all instruments.

In this example, we will set the DC power supply as our reference point. This VI and a previously created sub-VI are used to automatically set the DC power supply to six different voltages between 0 to 5 volts. These values are assumed to be our referenced values. Once our DC power supply is set to a given value, the VI will use NI DAQ and an Arduino to collect data simultaneously and present them in two different arrays that are recorded and presented on the Front Panel window. Although the focus here, in this book is on LabVIEW data acquisition, a developer must verify all data acquired (that is, against calculated or expected values); alternatively, as far as science and engineering are concerned, the developer should compare the data acquired against measurements acquired using a more precise measuring tool. This is why we will connect and visually observe (record) each set value by a FLUKE 117 as our most accurate device in the system.

Connections

1. Connect +/- from the DC Power supply to the main inputs of the Breadboard.
2. Connect FLUKE 117 Probe wires to the inputs of the breadboard.
3. Connect Arduino Ground to the negative (-) on the breadboard.

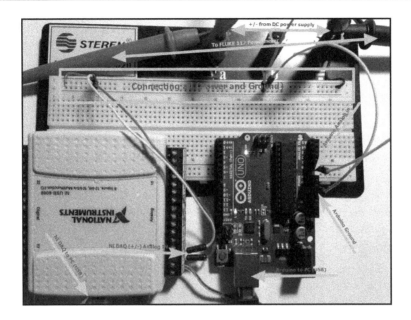

4. Connect Analog IN pin zero on the Arduino to breadboard (+).
5. Connect wires from the main input of the breadboard to (+/-) on the board.
6. Connect (+/-) on AI0 on the NI DAQ to the breadboard (+/-).
7. Connect the NI DAQ USB wire to the PC running LabVIEW.

LabVIEW block diagram

By now, the overall structure of all programs must shape a familiar trend.

Programs start by initializing, and then we enter a loop so that the main tasks of the program take place. And the last section involves performing the required clean up and stopping:

1. We need three serial connections through the USB port. We need to connect the DC power supply, an Arduino, and the NI UB DAQ to one PC. If your PC has enough USB ports, use them; otherwise any USB hub will do the job.
2. Create two serial port selectors and name them such that one is going to be used by Arduino and the other by the DC power supply. Make sure the operating system on the PC recognizes them and note the proper com number assigned to each device.

3. In this example, we are going to use a subVI we wrote previously. The sub-VI was called "serial_p_p (SubVI)". Locate the sub-VI and place it in the same folder as your current VI.

4. Place an "initialize" function from the LINX function platter.

5. Create a "For" loop, but do not connect any indexing number.

6. Create an array of strings and populate the array elements with the six commands VSET1:0.11 to VSET1:4.99 (the voltage values need not be the exact values on the following diagram, but they must be between 0-5).

7. Create two arrays of floating point numbers to initialize and store all values that the program will generate and display. We place them in the beginning of the loop and use "Shift Register" to build an array to store the acquired data into two different arrays. The content of each array is also displayed while the "For" loop is running.

8. Inside the "For" loop we have three cells of "Flat Sequence"; the reason for the sequence is to force a particular order of execution:

- Communicate with the DC power supply and set the output to the current value
- Delay about 1000 ms so that the DC supply stabilizes
- Read the value as Arduino measures it

9. Next we use DAQ Assistant to acquire data from NI USB-6008.

10. We convert the output from DAQ Assistant and populate the second array. The content of this array is also displayed.

11. Outside the "For " loop, we create a two-dimensional array from the output of the arrays we populated while inside the "For" loop.

12. Once again, we use our sub-VI to disconnect power from the DC power supply.

13. Finally, we close all open ports.

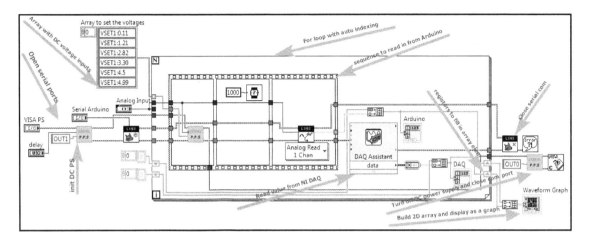

Front Panel

Your Front Panel should look very similar to the following figure. As always, before running the program, verify that the com ports chosen on the front panel match with what your operating system has assigned to each device.

The devices you use may not be exactly the ones used in this book. Values you collect are going to have small delta with the specific values recorded in this chapter.

Note the waveform graph resulting from the two sets of data acquired. It may not be appear at first glance, but there are two waveforms (one blue and one purple). Since the values are so close, they almost superimpose, but if you use different scales you will distinctly see the two different waveforms.

The difference is over 3-4%. This may be well within the tolerance of a certain project or may not be acceptable at all.

Also, see the following clip (`www.Put_URL_Here.come`). This clip depicts the measured DC power supply values, which in turn can be compared to those that are measured through NI DAQ and Arduino.

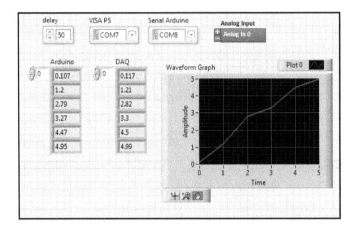

Summary

While traditional DAQs have played a detrimental role in the field of data acquisition, in recent years we have seen a surge of products that not only have surpassed in functionality and availability what was considered to be top-of-the-line just a few years back, but they also have added much more functionality at a lower price.

Among these newcomers, one family of products that has clearly gone above and beyond is the Arduino and Arduino-compatible boards and shields.

Digilent, which was recently acquired by National Instruments, produces higher-end boards compatible with the Arduino family of products. Although they are mainly produced to be utilized as microcontrollers, the fact of the matter is that they not only pack the capabilities of a DAQ, but they also bring many more functionalities that eliminate the requirement for extra hardware to complete a given job. We have examined serial communications, voltage manipulation, analog digital inputs and outputs, PWM, and an example that compares a traditional DAQ to an Arduino product. Speed and accuracy permitting, many of these open-sourced products can help the process of development and lower overall production and data acquisition.

7
Real-Time Issues

There are several issues that we all know about as they can happen to even the best of us. Needless to say, some of these incidents are completely out of our control and are OS and application related. We can be faced with losing a day's worth of work due to, for example, the infamous blue screen or an unexpected quit by an application.

The moral of the story is that while one cannot be too careful about each and every detail, unexpected issues still happen in "real time"! Given that all scientific practices, methods, precautions, and regular practice of backing up of all work done are tediously followed, there is always one major cause of havoc that cannot always be avoided; in one word, what an "upgrade" can do to your otherwise functioning system!

In this chapter, we will see how to avoid the following real-time issues.

Resolving upgradation issues

It is generally understood that a new version of software should have less bugs and more features and support a wider variety of hardware; or let us just assume so.

Compatibility

When software giants such as Microsoft plan an upgrade or a new version, usually they have been in contact with companies that use their product the most (that is, companies with the largest monetary income). They are aware of what those customers want and what has been missing, and of course, what bugs still remain to be fixed on the upcoming upgrade.

Deployment strategy

We will not go into too much detail on this subject, but imagine a factory that has hundreds or thousands of PCs and they all need to be upgraded. Suddenly a simple upgrade may cause down time and extra labor to ensure a smooth upgrade.

Backward compatibility

I did mention that you may need to upgrade all systems in a factory, but almost always NOT all systems do the exact same functionality and there are always a few that must keep backward compatibility. Most functionality created by the older version of the software must retain backward compatibility such that changes implemented on the new version may appear transparent to those systems.

Compatibility with another existing software application on a system

The hard fact is that most systems (hardware and software) introduced these days have not thoroughly gone through the classical definition of the software production cycle. The majority of cost saving and cuts have been on testing and at the same time they have shifted to automated testing. Many bugs escape inadequate automated testing these days more so than ever.

In real-time testing

Yet another somewhat different issue exists out there that more or less creeps into the categories I have been talking about in this chapter. Each measurement device has its own characteristics. Needless to say equipment used in a lab, a factory, or else out there in space, must be calibrated on a regular basis. Due to these characteristics being out of calibration, lack of precision, or simply "inaccurate" for specific test or data acquisition if you for instance connect a few different brands of voltmeters to a single source of current and voltage, the display of each of the devices should show the same value, but in reality this is not the case.

NI's native instruments

In previous chapters, we used Arduino hardware and unofficial LabVIEW software modules to illustrate the examples. While this approach has its few advantages (price and simplicity), Arduino in fact is more of a beginner's and hobbyist environment than a professional development platform. Ideally, we would prefer to use NI's native hardware and software. Software wise we have been talking about LabVIEW and there should be no doubt that LabVIEW can go head to head with any graphical programming environment that is out there. It is by far the most used in R&D, science, and academia.

Hardware wise

NI offers several categories of hardware to accommodate DAQ measurements. CompactDAQ, CompactRIO, Ethernet, PCI, PCI Express, PXI Platform SCXI, USB, and wireless products ensure data acquisition and measurement in almost any environment and situation. But in reality, with all the benefits that each and every one of these devices provide, there is a cost associated that must be taken into consideration.

While the cost of high-end hardware can be easily absorbed by professional companies, they are not within reach of individuals, students, and even academia. To resolve this problem, National Instruments has a solution.

National Instrument's myRIO-1900

LabVIEW is one of the four entities that construct LabVIEW **Reconfigurable I/O (RIO)**. The other three are a **processor**, **reconfigurable FPGA**, and **measurement I/O hardware**.

myRIO-1900 offers a student version of RIO:

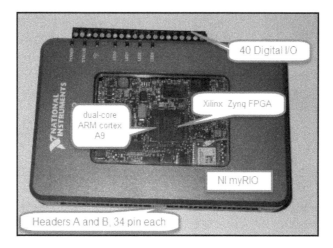

The NI myRIO-1900 provides **analog input (AI)**, **analog output (AO)**, **digital input and output (DIO)**, audio, and power output in a compact embedded device:

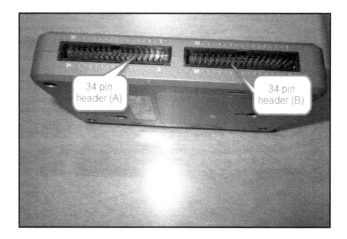

The NI myRIO-1900 connects to a host computer over USB and wireless 802.11b,g,n:

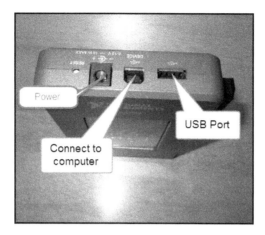

Along with this hardware, the following software must be installed before one can use myRIO:

The required software for programming myRIO:

- LabVIEW
- LabVIEW Real-Time Module
- LabVIEW myRIO Toolkit

The optional software for programming myRIO includes:

- LabVIEW FPGA Module
- Compilation Tools for Vivado
- Vision Development Module
- Vision Acquisition Software
- LabVIEW Control Design and Simulation Module
- Control Design Assistant
- System Identification Assistant
- LabVIEW MathScript RT Module
- LabVIEW Robotics Module for myRIO and roboRIO

Here is a screenshot of myRIO toolkit as modules shown in LabVIEW:

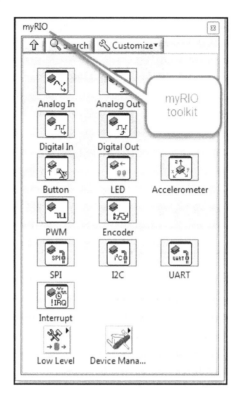

To conclude the discussion regarding the introduction of error by less expensive devices, here we have YU-2381BY, probably the smallest voltmeter in the world:

This particular version supports a voltage range of 2 to 30 volts:

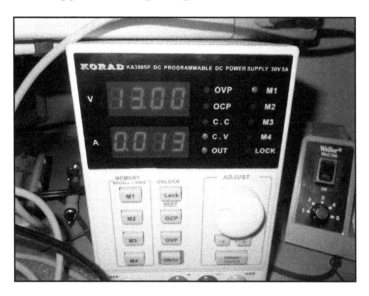

Note that at 13.00 volts, this device shows a voltage reading of 12.9:

Depending on your project a 0.1 difference might be negligible or detrimental!

Another area where major difficulties may arise is the actual parsing of returned data from instruments and measuring devices. Particularly at the design phase of a product, communication with the device is generally done using text commands. Given the fact that LabVIEW uses a graphical environment, LabVIEW developers must take extra steps to communicate with the device under development and most of the precision measurement devices. Considerable care must be taken to define the syntax, and detect the beginning and the end of prompts and commands to and responses from the device.

8

DAQ at a Distance - Network and Distributed Systems

Today we live in the age of networks to the extent that it is actually hard to find isolated islands with no network around. To take advantage of these networks is not only beneficial, but at times very necessary. After the initial setting, many of the adjustments and data collection can be performed remotely just outside the lab (with VPN and proper connections). In general, device manufacturers provide drivers for use by customers. National Instruments has taken downloading and installation of drivers, and more importantly version control of the drivers, and have made it even easier. LabVIEW version 8.5 and beyond is capable of acquiring and installing drivers from within LabVIEW. Since much of this (acquiring the drivers and installation) uses the Internet and local networks, it is worthwhile to dedicate a complete chapter to it.

In this chapter, we will learn:

- Developing and monitoring from a distance
- Distributed Test application using GPIB-ENET
- NI Distributed system manager
- NI Web publishing tool
- Configuring for DHCP, configuring for static IP address, and monitoring system resources and I/O

Verifying the computer's connection

It may sound trivial, and in most cases it is, but if this unit is being used in a professional company, it's IT department can be very helpful in case there are issues. But be aware that simple security (a username and password) will be required. We will verify that all connections and security are taken care of by simply looking for the device and verifying the local IP of the GPIB assigned to it by running GPIB Ethernet Wizard:

1. Launch NI Max and click on **Devices and Interfaces**.
2. Click on **Network Devices** on the left-hand pane.

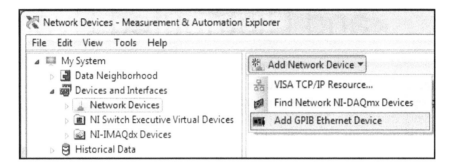

3. From the right-hand side drop-down menu click on **Add Network Device** and choose **Add GPIB Ethernet Device**. This will launch **NI-488.2**, the GPIB Ethernet Wizard.

4. Click on the **Next** button. This is the crucial point; that is, the software will start to search for connected devices. If all goes well you will see the list of detected devices or at least one device. But before looking at a successful search, let's look at the failure window. The window that appears when the wizard cannot find any device:

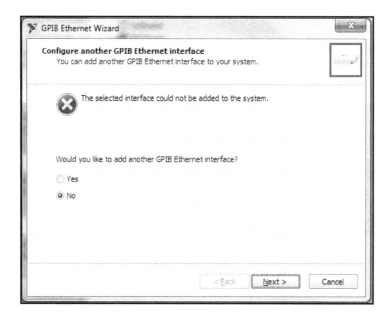

5. If you see the preceding window, obviously it means that no device is found, try the following:

    1. Power down all connected devices
    2. Power backup all devices
    3. Wait 90 seconds to a few minutes for the device to boot
    4. Verify the network connection

6. You may also need to make sure that your installed version of LabVIEW is running the web server. To verify, the inside LabVIEW from the **Tools** menu choose **Options**, then choose **Web Server**, and finally click on **OK**.

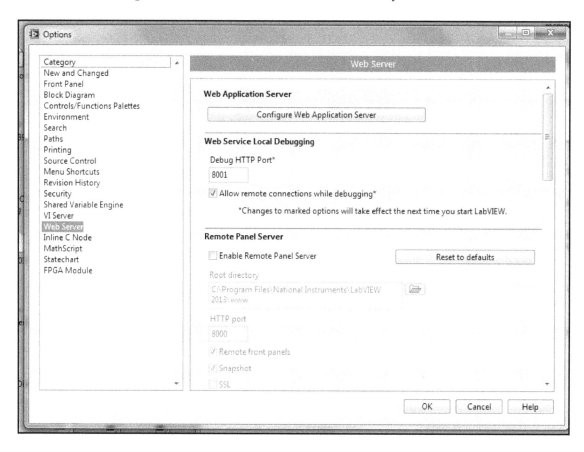

7. When NI MAX successfully finds at least one device, you will be presented with the following window:

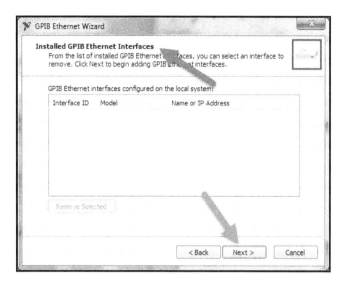

8. It then looks for the device in the local subnet. Press **Next** when the following window appears:

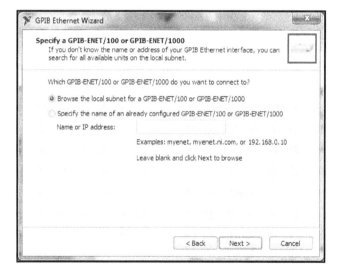

9. After browsing for available interfaces, if successful the following window appears:

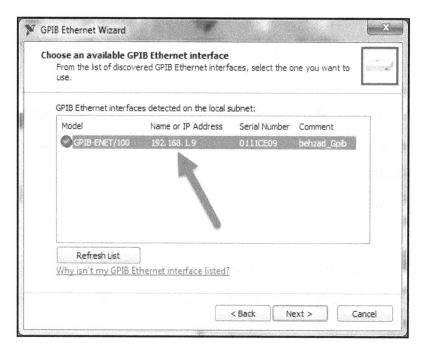

10. Note the local IP; in this example it is **192.168.1.9**. More importantly, note the serial number. This serial number must match the serial number printed on a label on the back of the device:

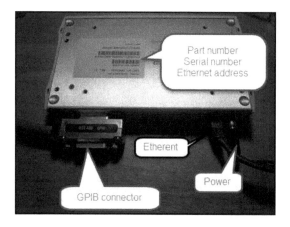

11. In the following window you are asked if you would like to configure another interface, choose **No** and press **Next** to continue.

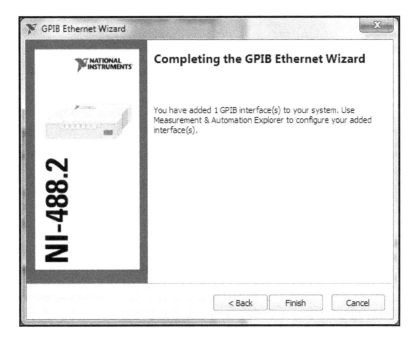

12. Finally, you are presented with a **Configuration Summary**. The Wizard will ask you **Would you like to use these settings?**, choose **Yes** and then click on **Next** and continue. Note the following:

    1. The IP address of the device.

    2. Note that "**Hostname**" is set to "**SR-NET**".

    3. This has been internally hardcoded:

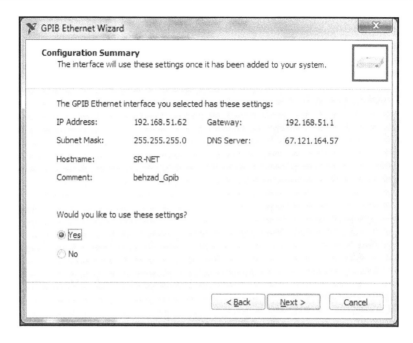

13. To verify proper communication (send and receive), and whether it is functioning correctly you may run a `ping` command on that IP address:
    1. Open a terminal window.
    2. Type `ping <IP address>`, as an example I typed `ping 192.168.9.1`.

14. You should get a response similar to the following window:

```
Microsoft Windows [Version 6.1.7601]
Copyright (c) 2009 Microsoft Corporation.  All rights reserved.

C:\Users\Ketab>ping 192.168.1.9

Pinging 192.168.1.9 with 32 bytes of data:
Reply from 192.168.1.9: bytes=32 time=1ms TTL=255
Reply from 192.168.1.9: bytes=32 time=3ms TTL=255
Reply from 192.168.1.9: bytes=32 time=1ms TTL=255
Reply from 192.168.1.9: bytes=32 time=1ms TTL=255

Ping statistics for 192.168.1.9:
    Packets: Sent = 4, Received = 4, Lost = 0 (0% loss),
Approximate round trip times in milli-seconds:
    Minimum = 1ms, Maximum = 3ms, Average = 1ms

C:\Users\Ketab>
```

15. Using NI MAX, this is the final configuration. Note that this example uses a **TDS 2022**. We have used this device in previous chapters. We will run an example towards the end of `Chapter 9`, *Alternate Software for DAQ*.

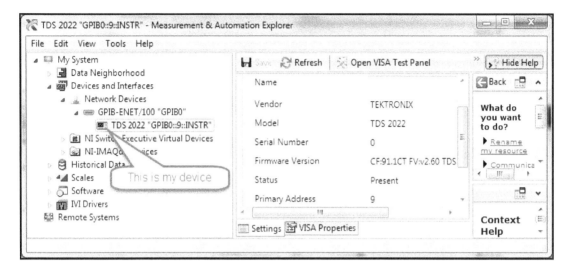

16. Right-click on the discovered device and choose **Properties**:

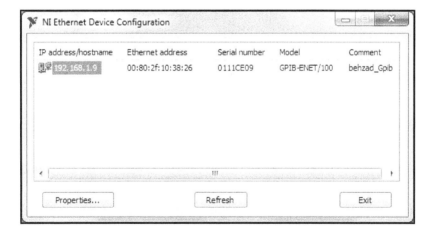

17. You should see the following window. Verify that the Serial number and Ethernet address matches that of actual hardware connected to the subnet.

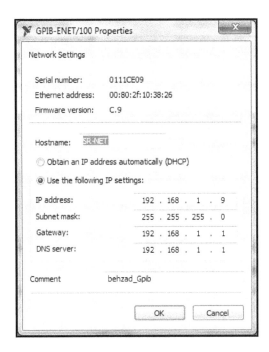

A distributed test application using GPIB-ENET

With the connections ready and everything set up, we will run a simple example. In this example, we will set the power supply to 2.3v DC and connect the DS 2022 leads to the power supply:

1. Launch LabVIEW, open a blank VI, and use Tektronix VI Tree. Drag and drop the following modules on the block diagram in the VI (see the block diagram of the following window):

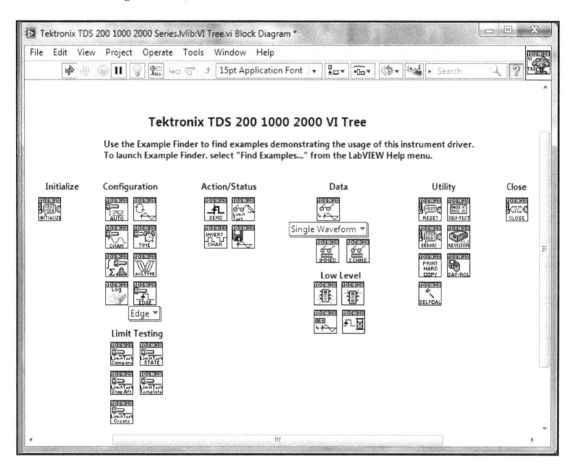

2. Connect all wires to have a complete VI, as depicted in the following screenshot:

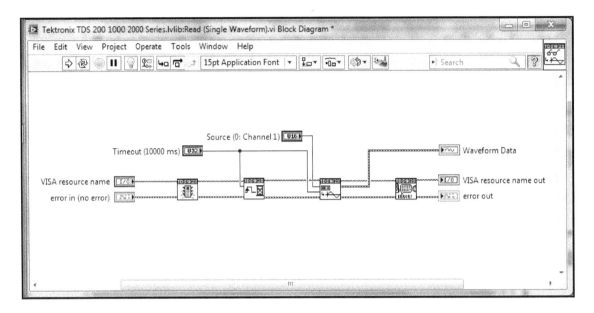

3. This will produce the following **Front Panel**:

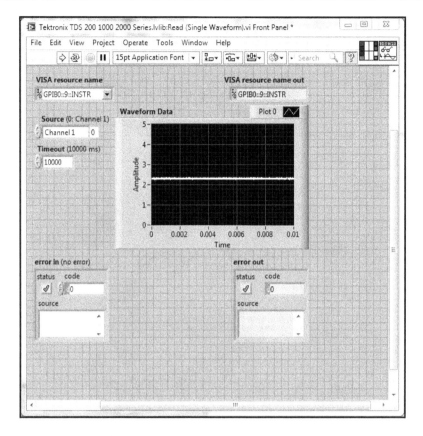

4. On the **Front Panel**, click on the arrow and choose the appropriate instrument:
    *   In our example, we have **GPIB0::9::INSTR**. Leave all other inputs with their default values.
    *   Press the Run arrow icon in the top left corner to execute the VI.
    *   LabVIEW chooses the X and Y limit values automatically and they change rapidly, sometimes so rapidly that one cannot see the correct trace that is drawn.

5. Right-click on the **Front Panel** window and choose to remove the automatic assignment of limits for the X and Y coordinates; enter an appropriate range. We are expecting to measure a 2.3v signal. So, setting the X coordinate limits to 0.00 to 5.00 should give us a good range view.

Handling errors

You may see the two following errors depending on your particular system or the devices and instruments you use. There are many devices and instruments out there and as stated at the beginning of the chapter, the content of this chapter can only be used as a guideline unless the user is employing the exact same hardware used in this chapter:

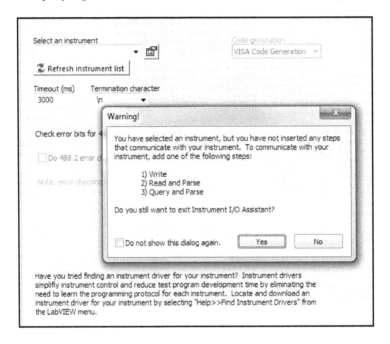

The second error:

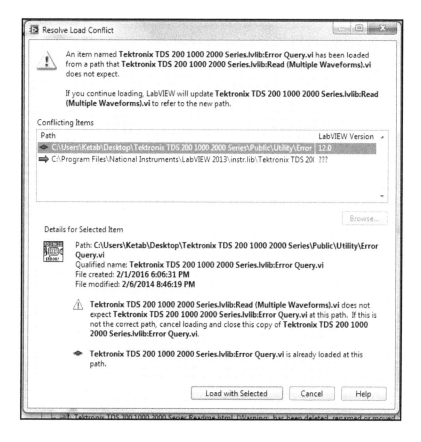

Summary

It has been years since tasks have been carried out remotely. LabVIEW is no exception. In this chapter, we showed how to use. Conet an ENET100 and we went through the connection step-by-step and verified each one.

Note that we used a local network. In a manufacturing or lab area, you may have to ask your network administrator to assign you a static one.

9
Alternate Software for DAQ

In the preceding chapters, we sat up our system in somewhat a "Lab" or hypothetical conditions; that is, we assumed that all necessary tools (hardware and software) are provided as we needed them. The second premise throughout those chapters was that our hypothetical goals would be completely fulfilled by what tools we used. In reality, in most cases we have to work in mixed mode situations where we do not have the luxury to need only "simple" measurements or to be able to use equipment all built by the same manufacturer (so that there would not be any cross incompatibility) and with all connections, cabling, and software working in perfect harmony; all using the latest and greatest versions of software without crashes, freezes, and blue screens.

In fact, in more cases than not, engineers need to work with systems that are all or partially inherited from other engineers or previous tasks and they include a mix of hardware and software. Obviously, there cannot be one single book that can cover all, even most, possible combinations of a system at any given time. This is neither possible (not even imaginable), nor has it been the intended aim of this book. Every test and measurement device manufacturer will test their own product to an extent and if we assume this amount of test is enough then what remains and pertains to this book would be to examine how a combination of hardware and software communicate with each other effectively and efficiently.

Industry direction

The falling rate of profit, and attempt to maximize profit, as well as technological innovations and a few other minor factors have forced manufacturers into two main directions:

- Standardization:

  No longer is it profitable to have components of a product to be built in-house by any given manufacture's own design and specifications where they would have to absorb the cost of R&D and manufacturing as well as maintaining a fleet of supporting factories for non-essential parts and segments of a product. It just cuts into profits and worse yet, others can do it better. As an example, Nikon can make the camera, but Leica M provides better lenses than Nikon can.

- Modulation:

  Effective modularization of a system, and portioning each device to a smaller daughterboard and sub system would vastly reduce the cost of remain and maintenance. Imagine data acquisition systems that have a main body and may be a single screen, but they can accommodate an array of modules. Such a system once configured properly can take the place of several legacy instruments.

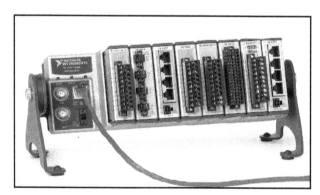

More complex systems, such as the one previously depicted, are also accompanied with a very capable software package, such as LabVIEW and TestStand, which has been the main topic of this book.

Missing from the LabVIEW arsenal

Communication is an essential part of data acquisition. It is well understood and adequate tools are provided with LabVIEW. But there is one area that LabVIEW needs to improve.

LabVIEW does not support secure transfer of data or files

But there is older, time tested, and mostly free software out there that might not be nearly as capable as proficiently supported software, but one should not underestimate the power and usefulness of software out there that can do a task very well and efficiently. Let's look at a few well known ones and see what they can do.

Serial terminal emulator software

Somewhere around 2001, the introduction of Windows XP by Microsoft was when Windows actually became useful for the main stream user (can anybody remember Windows 1 back in 1982 or Windows 3 in 1995?). **Hyper Terminal** introduced with Windows soon became a very useful tool to communicate with various instruments and devices.

Tera Term

Tera Term is a free and open-sourced communication software (Terminal Emulator). It can emulate DEC VT100 to DEC VT382. It also has support for telnet, SSH1 and SSH2, as well as serial port. It is capable of emulating different types of computer terminals, from DEC VT100 to DEC VT382. It supports telnet, SSH 1 and 2, and serial port connections. If you need Macros, there is one built-in.

While software like Tera Term is only a terminal emulator, there are many occasions where software files must be transferred through a network. **puTTY** is a collection of files that each do specific tasks very well, telnet, SSH, SFTP. PuTTY was originally developed by Simon Tatham for Windows.

Here are the PuTTY files according to the publisher:

- PuTTY (the SSH and Telnet client itself)
- PSCP (an SCP client, that is, command-line secure file copy)
- PSFTP (an SFTP client, that is, general file transfer sessions much like FTP)
- PuTTYtel (a Telnet-only client)
- Plink (a command-line interface to the PuTTY backends)
- Pageant (an SSH authentication agent for PuTTY, PSCP, PSFTP, and Plink)
- PuTTYgen (an RSA and DSA key generation utility)

Using manufacturer's instrument drivers (such as HP, Agilent):

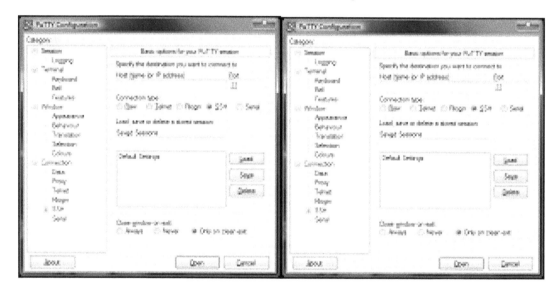

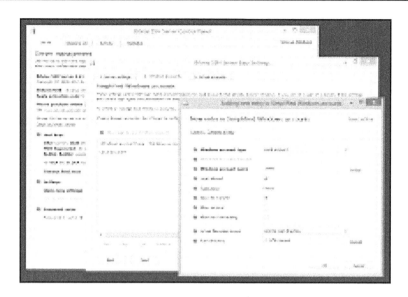

Measurement computing DASYLab

Measurement computing develops both software and hardware for data acquisition:

10
Non-National Instrument Devices DAQ

Before we start on the main topic, a few words of caution are necessary. Any work we do starts with electricity, and in particular, a power supply. I do realize I have mentioned power supplies in passing in such sentences as "set power supply to such and such volts….". But it suddenly dawned on me that (maybe it is because I have several power supplies scattered around my lab) power supplies deserve much more attention than I have given them so far. Choosing the correct power supply obviously depends on the range of use it will be used for (and of the cores of your budget). But just knowing this fact is not enough. Power supplies are used in two main categories: in a rack with several instruments in which they are set once, and not so often a technician or an engineer checks them as needed, the law requires that all instruments should be calibrated by independent companies once a year. This case mostly applies to factories. The other way power supplies are used is more or less R&D environments, by researchers, hobbyists, and makers, which usually means they are used by different people for much shorter times (compared to their use in factories). Hence many more adjustments to the device occurs. In this chapter, we will take a much closer look at power supplies.

Safety

I have always assumed that mentioning to adults "follow safety measures at all times" is somewhat condescending. Until one power supply blew up a few centimetres from my face. I was lucky that I did not get seriously hurt. But I have been in a laser lab where a technician did not use proper goggles and lost one of her eyes permanently.

So, use extra caution when working, building, or modifying a power supply to fit your exact project.

There are two major parts to any power supply

I suppose it is very obvious that any power supply has one input and one or more outputs. In the US, major appliance power suppliers accommodate for both 110 and 220 volts. Commercial power supplies (depending how much you are willing to pay) also accommodate for variable input and fixed or variable outputs. On a cautious note, newer power supplies automatically detect if the input is 110 or 220 volts. But there are still power supplies that one has to manually select one or another. Most recently, I have seen manual selection of input voltage in desktop computers.

A more correct name

A more correct name for what we are taking about is power adapters. At least we should be able to consider the distinction. Consider an electric iron. Here, the input voltage goes through a fuse and a couple of resistors, but it uses all of 110/ 120.

But an electric clock, digital TVs, and many more appliances use much less than 110/220 volts

Why such an introduction?

In this chapter, we will be talking about hardware made for use with LabVIEW by other companies (and not National Instruments). Almost any reputable company releases LabVIEW Vis with their hardware. Make sure to search for the LabVIEW drive and Vis. Our main component will be a measurement computing DAQ and several boards that are made to do certain specific jobs. We will talk extensively about the DAQ, but these boards I mentioned previously are also very good and better yet at very reasonable prices. They are Chinese made and you can buy some of them on Amazon and many more nice gadgets at h ttps://www.banggood.com. The two products we are going to use are:

E-1608, 16-Bit Multifunction Ethernet DAQ Device

Key highlights:

- 16-bit high-speed Ethernet device
- Sample rates up to 250 kS/s
- 8 SE/4 DIFF analog inputs
- Two 16-bit analog outputs
- Eight individually-configurable digital I/O
- One 32-bit counter input
- Includes a built-in 10/100 BASE-T auto-negotiation, high-speed communication port
- Uses TCP/IP and UDP for network communication
- Includes CAT-6 Ethernet cable and 5 V power supply adapter
- Screw-terminal connectors
- Board-only OEM version available
- Software support for DAQami data-acquisition companion software for acquiring data and generating signals
- TracerDAQ for acquiring and displaying data and generating signals
- Universal Library includes support for Visual Studio and Visual Studio .NET, including examples for Visual C++, Visual C#, Visual Basic, and Visual Basic .NET
- Universal Library for Android includes support and examples for the Android 3.1 platform (API level 12) and later
- DASYLab and NI LabVIEW drivers
- InstaCal software utility for installing, configuration, and testing

- Supported operating systems are Windows 10, 8, 7, and Vista, 32-bit or 64-bit
- Android 3.1 (API level 12) and later

USB-1608G Series

Key highlights:

- Average Rating: USB-1608G Series – 16-bit high-speed multifunction
- DAQ devices
- 16 analog inputs
- Up to 500 kS/s sample rate
- 8 digital I/O
- Up to two analog outputs
- Support for Windows, Linux, and Android

The simplest test

Trust me on this, every time you design, build, or make anything, the first and most important thing is to do the simplest test before anything else. This may sound (dare I say) foolish, but in my 35 years of working as a technician in a factory to a few R&D labs from a medical device company to Apple computers (and many other jobs in between), I have never seen a product go straight from design and build to use. What I mean is that if you make a radio, don't try to see if it gets fifty channels, before everything else see if it turns on, just turn it on and off a few times.

Now back to our main topic. I have one or more measurement computing DAQs. Although the main purpose is to use LabVIEW with these devices, first start by installing original software that comes with the device and see if the device is functioning as it should; from the MOST SIMPLE task to putting the device through the most complicated ones for a long period of time. Another point to consider is: do not be satisfied if a device works for a few minutes or hours. Do a real long time test, depending on what "long" means according to the device. A long time means one thing for a light bulb and another to a laser device!

Did you know about these gems!

I discovered several Chinese companies that make very small "electronic modules" at a very reasonable price. Don't misunderstand me, the quality is good. I have been using this power adapter (110v to 5v) for some time now. This is about the size of two quarters:

A simple test of MC DAQ 1608G

Maybe I have said this in different words earlier, but here is another version. Data acquisition is in essence measuring voltages and currents and translating them to final need or use. When you flip a switch to turn on or off a light, you are sending a certain amount of electricity to the light bulb (not much manipulation here), but what happens when you press a key on a keyboard is the same (you press a key and with much manipulation, a character appears on the screen).

Here I have plugged the DAQ into my computer via a USB cable and set the output via input LabVIEW module to 7.5Volts (of course I started from much lower voltages):

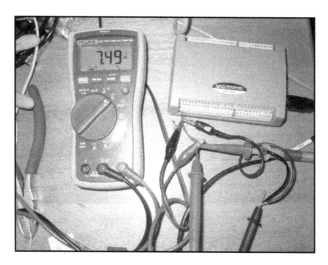

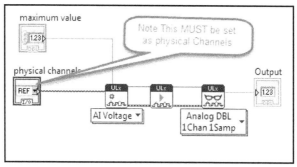

I set up the preceding diagram and tested the USB DAQ. A simple test, but all went well. Pay attention to the fact that these are polymorphic modules and you need to tweak the modules:

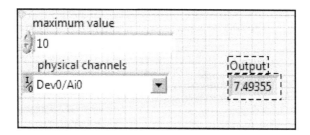

Two important notes about the preceding example, the cores are not so important "everywhere", but I have set my (semi) expensive power supply to 20 volts and expect a certain amount of accuracy (FLUKE 117 IS very accurate), but it shows an output of 19.99 volts. The most important aspect to consider is that (remember I have been using DAQ accompanying CD that is shipped with the MC DAQ 1608G) once you install the LabVIEW modules, you can work in LabVIEW.

I did talk about the adjustable power supply AC to DC converter in earlier chapters. Although that one is necessary, it is not enough, and being relatively expensive, we all agree it is best to have many of those, but they only can be found in a few "privileged" labs. For the rest of us there are many less expensive ones. Surprisingly, these power supplies/adapters are much more accurate than I thought. The limitations of these less expensive power supplies/adapters are in their flexibility, and the number of functionality and the amount of load they can take is still very useful.

Let's take a short look at a couple of them.

MB-102 MB102 Solderless Breadboard, power supply, and jumper cable

Most designs are now done in a variety of the software that is available for almost any job. But there are occasions that actual electronic components need to go on a breadboard and designs need to be a fine-tuned manually. For the price, this is a good one and mine has been working reliably for a year:

Where else can you get a 1 x MB-102 Solder less Breadboard, 1 x MB-102 power supply plus 65 Breadboard jumper cables, and a nice breadboard? This one connects to a wall socket and supplies 3 to 5 volts to both sides of a breadboard. This makes working on the breadboard very easy as far as having access to power.

E-1608 – 16-Bit multifunction Ethernet DAQ device

As the name suggests, E-1608 is the Ethernet counter part of a USB-1608G device. Software installation of E1608 is also a bit non-conventional. The software is divided into several pieces and it has to answer yes or no to the question of do you want to install this software? The confusing part is that unless you are very familiar with the MC DAQ then there is no way for you to know if the answer should be yes or no. So you install everything. Of course there is no simple or different answer to this dilemma. I suppose given that people have many terabytes of hardware space, my personal preference would be to install everything in the beginning and once the user is well familiar with the hardware and software, then they can delete what is not needed. I suppose Microsoft and National Instruments are doing this (of course to those parts of software that they can't charge the customer extra money for) Microsoft and National instruments are somewhat doing this Ethernet or USB or CD) are not the only difference. Measurement computing lists the capabilities of the E-1608:

- 16-bit high-speed Ethernet device
- 8 SE/4 DIFF analog inputs
- Two 16-bit analog outputs
- Eight individually-configurable digital I/O
- One 32-bit counter input
- Includes a built-in 10/100 BASE-T auto-negotiation, high-speed communication port
- Uses TCP/IP and UDP for network communication
- Includes CAT-6 Ethernet cable and 5 V power supply adapter
- Screw-terminal connectors

To use the Ethernet version, one must connect the hardware and then install the software. This way the software will be able to discover the hardware and configure it. As with other networked devices, setting up the Ethernet version is much more complex than the USB version.

The following is an image of an Ethernet version. Note the green and orange lights around the Ethernet cable. Once both the power and the Ethernet cable are connected, it takes a few minutes for the device to be recognized by the network and be seen by any user of the local, notice "local network", and only one person can use the device at any given time:

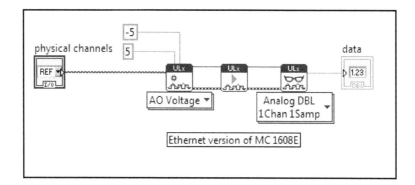

LabVIEW obviously runs the preceding diagram only once. A couple things must be taken care of before the VI can run. On "physical channels" the device must be selected. If you are not familiar with the device, you should pick the first option that Windows and MC has assigned to the device. In my case, it has always been "Dev0/Ai0". But on many occasions, the following warning box appears:

Although not shown in the preceding example, a "clear" module should be placed before the end of the VI.

An important message for LabVIEW users: MC has its own software to run MC DAQs. Although these modules appear in the LabVIEW list of modules, in several cases a strange message appears that "Not all functionality of this module is available in LabVIEW!!".

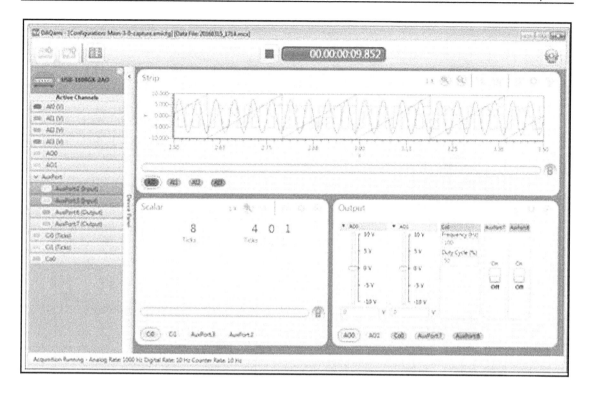

Summary

I suppose I have listed many shortcomings of MC DAQ and Universal Libraries since my point of view is LabVIEW and non-National Instruments can and would do the job. But in fact, MC with its own software, DAQami and DASYLab, and DAQ hardware will be useful to many engineers and technicians.

I have not had the chance to use DAQAmi, but it appears to be a very powerful software.

11
LabVIEW and Simple Microcontrollers

It was not too long ago that microcontrollers only handled digital I/O. Now, we are just celebrating the tenth anniversary of Arduino-compatible microcontrollers and a slew of other platforms such as Raspberry Pi that have A/D and D/A, memory, UART, USB, and I2C bus.

These *open platforms* have spun a huge industry that includes hundreds of add-ons called **shield**, which enhance the original capabilities of these microcontrollers. Combined with these microcontrollers and a fairly simple development environment, these boards have created capabilities for these products to be a test and possibly development platforms that may provide the functionality of the much more expensive DAQs. Obviously, simplicity and much lower monetary values of these platforms are exchanges made with precision, documentation, and inherent limitation of these devices.

An Arduino Uno Rev3, the most recent of Arduino products and compatible product families (known as shields) and Digilent's ChipKit Uno32, a 32-bit MIPS processor core development board that is in the same form factor of the original Arduino Uno product family.

DAQ devices versus microcontrollers

It is now almost over a decade and a half since microcontrollers have no longer been limited to digital I/Os. Mixed signals, control bus memory, separate timers, and counters have pushed their way into traditional microcontrollers with a speed that is only limited by the die size and functionality required, and most certainly price.

It is an undisputable fact that in data acquisition, speed and accuracy are directly related to the actual hardware and processors used and, depending on the speed and accuracy intended, a user must use proper hardware/software. In other words, proper instrumentation is the *key* to meaningful Data Acquisition. However, speed and accuracy at any given time in history have been relative terms. The terms high speed and accuracy have been highly relative throughout recent years and what we mean by speed and accuracy today is far different from what they meant just a few years ago.

Using the Arduino as a DAQ with LabVIEW

There are compelling reasons why a LabVIEW developer or tester may want to consider using these new low-cost microcontrollers (such as the Arduino family of products) as opposed to expensive (therefore, much more accurate) hardware:

- A vast area in development can be bypassed, at least in the early stages with off-the-shelf, less expensive, and open source hardware.
- Not everyone needs top-of-the-line, the fastest, or the greatest (at any given time), hardware.
- These platforms are by design, expandable, upgradable, and widely available. Supporting shields that are also widely available, if they can be used, drastically reduces development time.
- And the most compelling reason, as far as the subject of this book is concerned, is that National Instrument's LabVIEW has been supporting these products for many years now. In fact, the second generation of firmware/development the VI library, which supports these products, has been released under LINX 1.0

Installing the Arduino firmware

To use the Arduino family of products in general, one must install its firmware using Arduino development environment. The original Arduino development software is a text-based environment similar to many other traditional development environments. NI LabVIEW interface for Arduino ToolKit (http://sine.ni.com/nips/cds/view/p/nid/209835) originally opened the door to LabVIEW users to program directly in LabVIEW. Although very useful, this toolkit still requires installation of LIFA, by an external program to LabVIEW. Introduction of LINX has been a major improvement over the original Arduino ToolKit.

Index

www.ingramcontent.com/pod-product-compliance
Lightning Source LLC
Chambersburg PA
CBHW060147060326
40690CB00018B/4010